An Encyclop of
Wool Embroidery
HERBS · GRASSES · FLOWERS

Acknowledgements

Dedication
To Margaret Kreft editor and friend.

Embroiderer: Merrilyn Heazlewood
Editor: Margaret Kreft
Illustrator: Sarah Sargison
Photographer: John de la Roche
Table Conversions: Sue Alexander
Graphic Designer: Patrick Badger
Pre-press: Crystal Graphics
Printing: Focal Printing

Published by Merriwood Press Pty Ltd
PO Box 306, Kingston, Tasmania, Australia 7051
Telephone: 61 (0)3 6229 8161
Fax: 61 (0)3 6229 8162
E-mail: lnielsen@heazlewood.com
Internet: http://www.heazlewood.com

ISBN 0 646 28756 7
First published 1997
Copyright © Merrilyn Heazlewood 1997.

All rights reserved.

No part of this publication may be reproduced, stored in or introduced into a retrieval system or transmitted in any form or by means (electronic, mechanical, photocopying, recording or otherwise) without prior written permission of the copyright owner. The designs in this book are published for the use of private individuals. Exploitation of them for commercial gain is prohibited and would infringe the copyright reserved above.

Other Titles by Author

 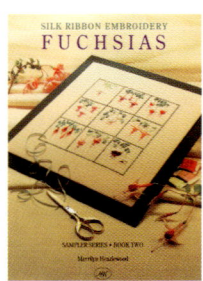 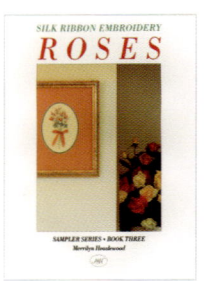 

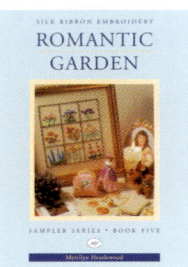 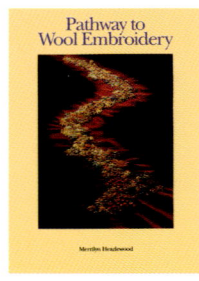 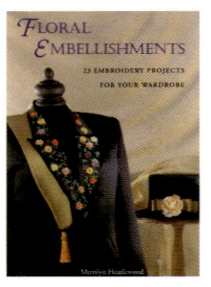 

Contents

5
Dear Embroiderer

6
General Information

11
Spring Bulbs and Cottage Garden Flowers

39
Herbs and Grasses

53
Australian Natives and North American Wildflowers

67
Blossom Garland, Roses, Fuchsia and Wisteria Garland

89
Stitch glossary

93
Index of Plants

95
Author Profile

Plants photographed on front cover

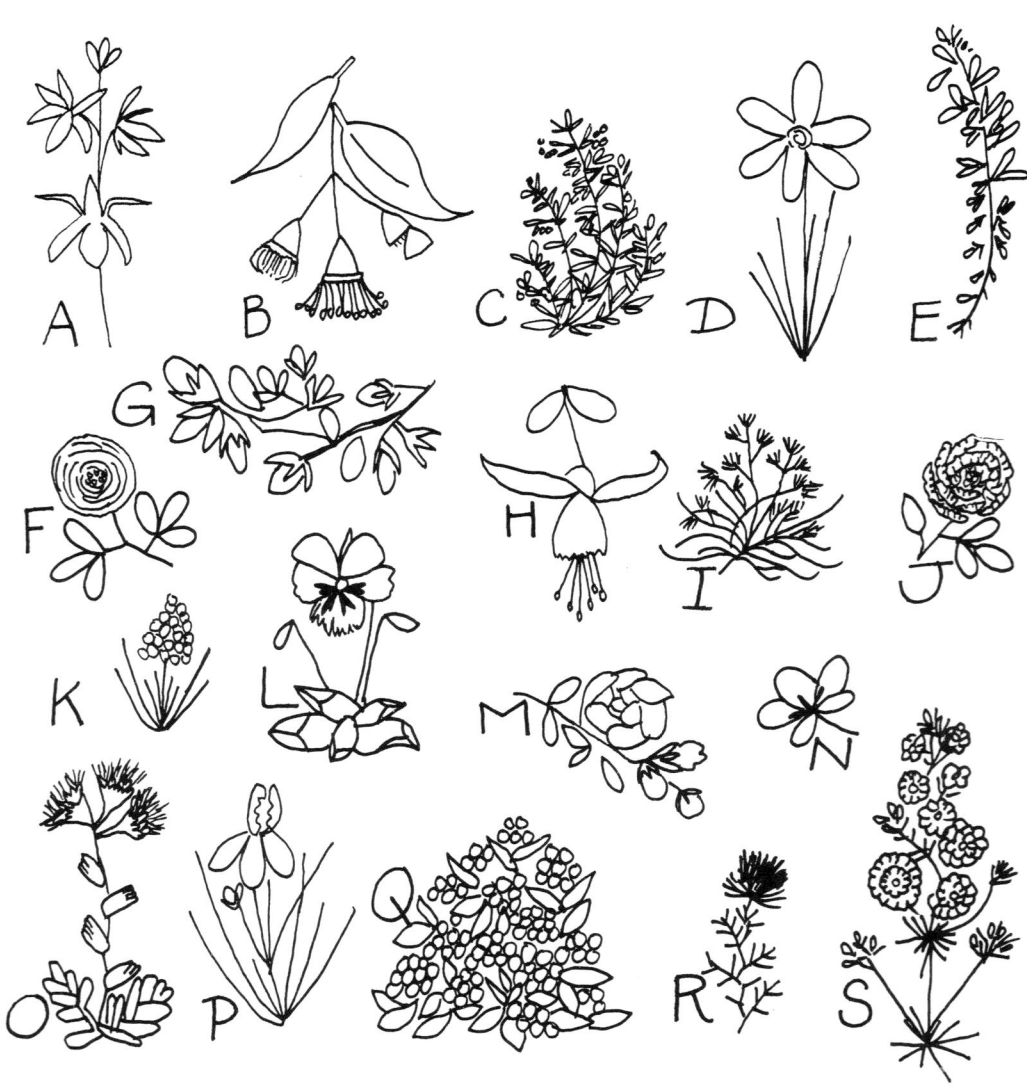

A. Cardinal (113)   B. Flowering Gum (94)   C. Rosemary (68)   D. Pheasants Eye (6)
E. Wisteria (177)   F. 'Woven' roses (138)   G. Blossom Bud (118)   H. Fuchsia (173)
I. Meadow Grass (85)   J. 'Bullion' Rose (158)   K. Grape Hyacinth (4)   L. Viola (34)
M. Blossom (121)   N. Rose (150)   O. Cotton Weed (36)   P. Iris (14)
Q. Hydrangea (45)   R. Thistle (41)   S. Larkspur (60)

Dear Embroiderer,

Wool has been a part of my life for as long as I can remember. My mother and grandmothers hand-knitted and embellished my baby clothes. My baby blanket (so my mother tells me) had on it the most beautiful embroidery. As a toddler it would still go everywhere with me until it was finally worn down to a corner! Some of my first attempts at wool embroidery were 'performed' on my doll's clothes.

Wool in its natural form was an integral part of my childhood. I remember being allowed one pet lamb per spring. I have memories of 'shadowing' my father as he shepherded the various flocks and breeds of sheep on our farm. Shearing time meant helping with the feeding of the shearers and delivering their morning and afternoon teas to the shearing shed. Occasionally, I was allowed to jump into the bags of shorn wool and press down the fleeces so that more could be put into the large bags. The distinct aroma of freshly shorn wool always reminds me of my happy and contented childhood spent growing up on the farm.

Spring brought the delights of new lambs and the re-appearance of the spring bulbs planted around the houses (those still being lived in and those long demolished) plus rows of bulbs along the farm lanes. From early spring our garden would burst forth with a multitude of cottage garden flowers, roses, fuchsias, wisteria and spring blossoms.

Spring was also grass time. I remember the calming effect of walking through paddocks with the 'swish swish' of the grasses swaying behind me. The various grasses I have designed for you in this Encyclopedia were also part of daily farm conversation as my father and brothers developed a grass seed growing, cleaning and exporting sector of the farm.

We always had herbs growing in our garden and I was frequently sent to pick a fresh bunch. Herbs are now part of my garden and we all know the richness of cooking with freshly picked herbs.

With such wonderful memories and experiences it has been a pleasure and a challenge to design and stitch for you the 178 plants in this Encyclopedia.

The section on Australian Native and North American Wildflowers is for those who have enjoyed my previous books. On my many visits to the USA and recent visit to Canada it has been a delight to see flowers that we grow in our Australian gardens growing wild on the side of the road, and to see flowers that we do not grow in Australia such as the shooting star and trillium.

With the warmth of wool, happy stitching,

General Information

Wools

Wool embroidery is a very quick and rewarding way to embroider your favourite flower or plant. In this Encyclopedia I have used crewel wools (also known as embroidery wools) and tapestry wools. Crewel wools are much finer than tapestry wools. Each brand of wool has its own shade range, thickness and degree of twist.

Crewel and Tapestry Wools

The crewel wools I have used are Appletons, DMC Medici, Gumnut, Paterna (one strand) and RoyalStitch. DMC Medici is the finest of the crewel wools. Always use one strand of crewel wool unless indicated otherwise.

The tapestry wools I have used are Appletons, DMC and Anchor. Appletons is the finest of the tapestry wools.

As you can see on the opposite page I have worked nine iris plants in different brands and styles of wool. I have done this to show you how the size of the flowers vary when using different wools.

If the wool I have used is not available refer to the conversion table on the same page and find a corresponding wool to use.

Variegated Wools

I have used variegated wools (Gumnut and RoyalStitch) in this Encyclopedia because the subtle colour changes result in a 'more realistic' embroidered plant such as the petunia (no. 38) and hydrangea (no. 45) on page 15.

The soft shade changes of variegated wools allow for the herbs, grasses and flowers to be natural in their appearance without having to change colours of wool.

Wool embroidery made easy

- When embroidering, the thread can twist or unravel. This is very frustrating. The reason is that you have threaded the needle with the 'wrong' end of the wool.

- Depending on the fabric I either:
  – tie a knot in the end of the wool before I embroider; or
  – if I am working on a woollen blanket (or a thick fabric) I 'run' the wool through a small area at the back of the fabric, then embroider over it.

- Once I have some embroidery worked, I 'run and weave' through the back of the embroidery to finish or start the length of wool.

- If you have embroidered an item that will get a lot of wear and laundering you may prefer to end off with a knot.

- No matter what style of fabric you wish to work on, be it synthetic or natural, the most important point to remember is that the fabric must open up easily for you when your needle is being pulled through. Bear in mind your needle may be large and holding a thick thread such as tapestry wool.

- If you are working on a fabric or garment which may pucker or stretch as you embroider, iron on some stabiliser before you begin. Complete the embroidery and then cut away the excess stabiliser.

Finishing Touches

When I was designing the plants for this Encyclopedia, I wanted to enhance the flowers which are all stitched in wool. I found I could achieve this by using other mediums. If you would prefer to work the flowers and plants in just wool then please do so.

I used silk ribbon for many of the leaves such as the viola (no. 34) on page 15. Sparkling organdy ribbon added 'fluffiness' to the blossom (no. 121) on page 69. The stamens on the fuchsias (nos 170–175) on page 72 were worked with stranded cotton. Perle cotton has been used for stems and leaves such as the hollyhock (no. 46) on page 16.

Fabrics

Wool embroidery can be worked onto all types of fabric.

I have completed projects of wool embroidery on fabrics such as wool, wool blends, cotton, linen, velvet, satin, and hand-knitted and machine-knitted garments. These fabrics were selected from fabric ranges made for use as clothing, soft furnishings (décor items), patchwork, quilting and embroidery.

In this Encyclopedia I have used cream gabardine and navy damask. Damask is available as a curtain fabric and a patchwork and quilting fabric. I used the latter as it is a lighter-weight damask.

Placement Guide

If the use of a placement guide will assist you, you may like to try one of the following:
- fine lead pencil;
- dressmaker's chalk;
- transfer pencil to make your own transfer;
- tacking or running stitch with fine sewing thread;
- 'rub-out' quilting pencil; or
- water-erasable or fade-away pens (I suggest minimal use of these items as they do not always 'disappear'!).

Needles

I worked with the following needles:
- crewel size 3 with Gumnut;
- crewel size 4 with Appletons;
- crewel size 5 with DMC Medici; and
- chenille size 20 with tapestry wool.

Remember that in a packet of mixed needles the lowest number refers to the largest needle.

Working Frames and Thimbles

I use a frame when working on smallish pieces of fabric i.e. cushion or pillow size. I work with either a Klipfast (Q-snap) square quilting frame or a small embroidery hoop. Quilting hoops can also be used.

When you are working with an embroidery or quilting hoop it is advisable to cover the inner ring by wrapping it with bias binding or fabric tape.

If you prefer to work without a hoop or frame please do, but I believe the finished result of working with a frame is better.

You may find, as I do, that it is advisable to use a thimble when embroidering on a firm fabric (tightly woven) and/or using a fine-'eyed' needle.

Scissors

Always use good quality, sharp embroidery scissors when embroidering. There is a large range for you to select from with different length blades. When embroidering with wool I prefer to use medium- to long-bladed embroidery scissors.

Laundering

I have hand washed and machine washed wool embroidery successfully in cold or tepid water with a mild soap/powder. I always make sure the garment/piece is well rinsed. Always take note of the laundering instructions for the fabric you have embroidered onto.

Due to the stricter environmental laws nowadays, the strong chemicals that were used to set 'dyes' may not always be used now. Hence, there is no guarantee that any thread (wool, cotton or silk) is totally dye fast, so please pre-wash strong colours to see that no excess dye comes out when laundered.

Spring Bulbs

Cottage Garden Flowers

SPRING BULBS
1. Jonquil
2. Iris
3. Snowflake
4. Grape Hyacinth
5. Cottage tulip
6. Pheasants Eye
7. Hyacinth
8. Daffodil
9. Hooped Petticoat
10. Crocus
11. Bluebell
12. Triple Layer Jonquil
13. Tulip
14. Iris
15. Narcissus

1. Jonquil	2. Iris	3. Snowflake	4. Grape Hyacinth	5. Cottage tulip
6. Pheasants Eye	7. Hyacinth	8. Daffodil	9. Hooped Petticoat	10. Crocus
11. Bluebell	12. Triple Layer Jonquil	13. Tulip	14. Iris	15. Narcissus

COTTAGE GARDEN 1
16. Forget-me-not
17. Calla Lily
18. Violet
19. Snapdragon
20. English Daisy
21. Aquilegia
22. Gentian
23. Primula
24. Sweet Pea
25. Pansy
26. Dianthus
27. Lilium
28. Geranium
29. Primrose
30. Morning Glory

16. Forget-me-not	17. Calla Lily	18. Violet	19. Snapdragon	20. English Daisy
21. Aquilegia	22. Gentian	23. Primula	24. Sweet Pea	25. Pansy
26. Dianthus	27. Lilium	28. Geranium	29. Primrose	30. Morning Glory

COTTAGE GARDEN 2
31. Scabious
32. Evening Primrose
33. Cyclamen
34. Viola
35. Fritillary
36. Cotton Weed
37. Heather
38. Petunia
39. Wallflower
40. Clematis
41. Thistle
42. Dahlia
43. Gladioli
44. Dandelion
45. Hydrangea

31. Scabious	32. Evening Primrose	33. Cyclamen	34. Viola	35. Fritillary
36. Cotton Weed	37. Heather	38. Petunia	39. Wallflower	40. Clematis
41. Thistle	42. Dahlia	43. Gladioli	44. Dandelion	45. Hydrangea

COTTAGE GARDEN 3
46. Hollyhock
47. Delphinium
48. Foxglove
49. Queen Anne's Lace
50. Michaelmas Daisy
51. Ragwort
52. Astilbe
53. Agapanthus
54. Lythrum
55. Tiger Lily (Turk's Cap)
56. Alkanet
57. Lupin
58. Japanese Anenome
59. Japanese Iris
60. Larkspur

46. Hollyhock	47. Delphinium	48. Foxglove	49. Queen Anne's Lace	50. Michaelmas Daisy
51. Ragwort	52. Astilbe	53. Agapanthus	54. Lythrum	55. Tiger Lily (Turk's Cap)
56. Alkanet	57. Lupin	58. Japanese Anenome	59. Japanese Iris	60. Larkspur

Spring Bulbs

Cottage garden 1

Cottage garden 2

Cottage garden 3

1. Jonquil

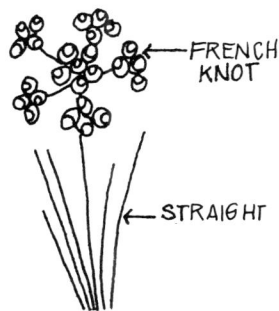

Stems and Leaves
Gumnut: green 586

Flowers
Gumnut: yellow 726; orange 809

1. Work the flowers in yellow, double-twist French knots.
2. Work the orange centre in a double-twist French knot.
3. Work the stems and leaves in straight stitches.

2. Iris

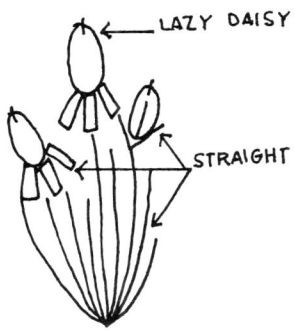

Stems and Leaves
RoyalStitch: green EW50

Flowers
Gumnut: pink 054; dark pink 057

1. Form the top petals with a pink lazy daisy using two strands of wool.
2. Form the lower petals with three, dark pink straight stitches using two strands of wool.
3. Work the bud in a pink, lazy daisy with a straight stitch centre.
4. Work the stems and leaves in straight stitches.

3. Snowflake

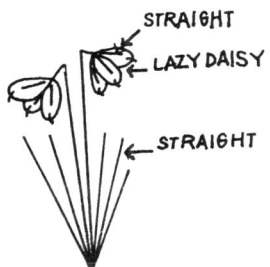

Stems and Leaves
Gumnut: green 615

Flowers
Gumnut: white 990; green 615

1. Form the flower with three lazy daisies with straight stitch centres.
2. Work the tip of each petal in a very, very, small straight stitch in green.
3. Work the stems and leaves in straight stitches.

DMC Medici	Gumnut	Paterna	RoyalStitch	Appletons Crewel	DMC Tapestry	Anchor Tapestry	Appletons Tapestry
8151	**054**	904	NC	753	7151	8454	753
8155	**057**	902	NC	755	7602	8368	755
8413	**586**	613	NC	425	7384	9016	425
8342	**615**	692	NC	543	7771	9096	543
8326	**726**	703	NC	472	7504	8134	472
8940	**809**	853	NC	441	7919	8166	441
white	**990**	261	NC	991B	white	8004	991B
8415	541	D501	**EW50**	832	7956	8966	832

4. Grape Hyacinth

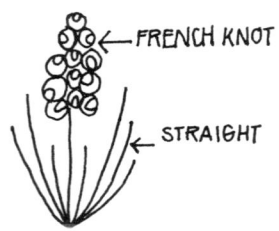

Stem and Leaves
Gumnut: green 586

Flower
Gumnut: dark blue 389

1. Form the flower with single-twist French knots using two strands of wool.
2. Work the stems and leaves in straight stitches.

5. Cottage Tulip

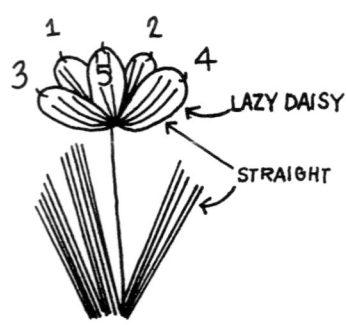

Stem and Leaves
RoyalStitch: green EW50

Flower
Gumnut: red 038; yellow 726

1. Work the stem in a straight stitch.
2. Work the petals in red lazy daisies as shown in the diagram. Fill in with straight stitches mixing red and yellow.
3. Form each leaf with five, long straight stitches worked closely together.

6. Pheasants Eye

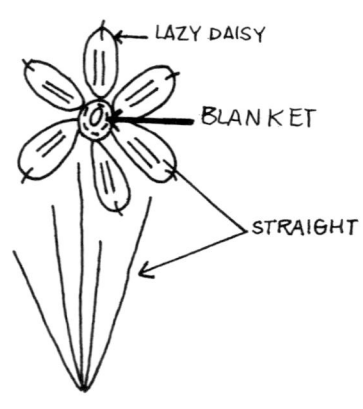

Stem and Leaves
RoyalStitch: green EW50

Flower
Gumnut: white 990; lemon 745
DMC stranded cotton: rust 349

1. Work the stem and leaves in straight stitches.
2. Work the petals in white, long lazy daisies with two straight stitches inside each lazy daisy.
3. Form the trumpet by working a small circle of lemon, blanket stitch. Whip over the top edge of the trumpet with one strand of rust cotton.

7. Hyacinth

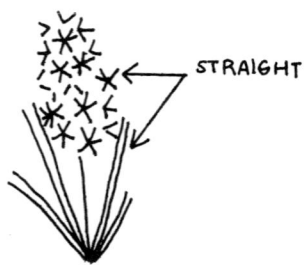

Stem and Leaves
Gumnut: green 586

Flower
Gumnut: blue 386

1. Form the stem with a straight stitch.
2. Work the flowerets in the middle with six small straight stitches.
3. Work the flowerets at the side and top of the plant with one, two or three, small straight stitches.
4. Form the leaves with two straight stitches worked closely together.

8. Daffodil

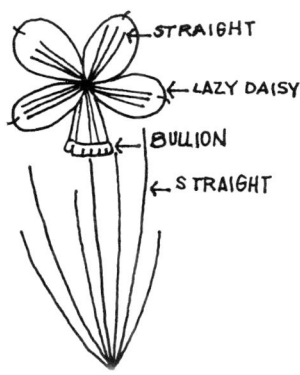

Stem and Leaves
Gumnut: green 586

Flower
Gumnut: yellow 726; orange 809

1. Work the stem and leaves in straight stitches.
2. Work the petals in four, yellow lazy daisies with three straight stitches in the centre of each lazy daisy.
3. Form the trumpet with five, orange straight stitches placed closely together then work a ten-wrap bullion at the end of the trumpet.

9. Hooped Petticoat

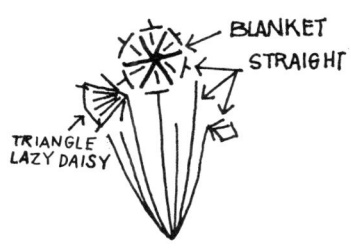

Stems and Leaves
Gumnut: green 615

Flowers and Bud
RoyalStitch: dark yellow EW70

1. Work the stems in straight stitch.
2. Form the 'facing' flower trumpet with a circle of blanket stitch and work the petals in small straight stitches.
3. Work the 'side-view' flower trumpet in a triangle lazy daisy filled in with four straight stitches. Work the petals in straight stitches as shown in the diagram.
4. Work the bud, bud 'greenery' and leaves in straight stitches.

10. Crocus

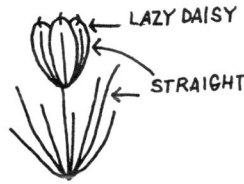

Stem and Leaves
Gumnut: green 586;
light lilac 255

Flower
Gumnut: light lilac 255

1. Work the stem in a lilac straight stitch.
2. Work the flower in three lazy daisies with straight stitch centres.
3. Work the leaves in straight stitch.

DMC Medici	Gumnut	Paterna	RoyalStitch	Appletons Crewel	DMC Tapestry	Anchor Tapestry	Appletons Tapestry
8103	**038**	970	NC	502	7666	8202	502
8332	**255**	334	EW33	884	7241	8584	884
8798	**386**	544	EW40	462	7798	8688	462
8720	**389**	541	NC	464	7797	8690	464
8413	**586**	613	NC	425	7384	9016	425
8342	**615**	692	NC	543	7771	9096	543
8326	**726**	703	EW70	472	7504	8134	472
8026	**745**	727	EW70	741	7503	8058	741
8940	**809**	853	NC	441	7919	8166	441
white	**990**	261	NC	991B	white	8004	991B
8415	541	D501	**EW50**	832	7956	8966	832
8026	745	727	**EW70**	741	7055	8058	741

Spring Bulbs

11. Bluebell

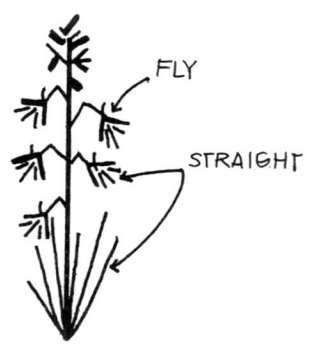

Stem and Leaves
Gumnut: green 586

Flowers
Gumnut: lilac 273

1. Work the stem in a straight stitch.
2. As shown in the diagram work small, green straight stitches to attach the flowers to the stem.
3. Form each flower by working a 'wide' fly stitch. Work a long straight stitch in the centre and two shorter straight stitches either side.
4. Work the leaves in straight stitch.

12. Triple Layer Jonquil

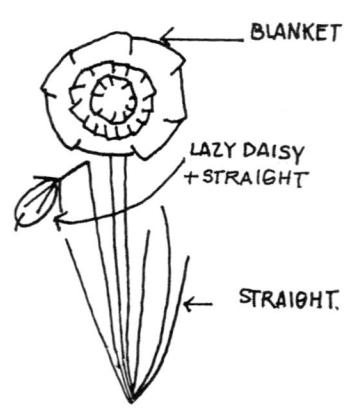

Stems and Leaves
Gumnut: green 615

Flower and Bud
RoyalStitch: dark yellow EW70
Gumnut: yellow 726; cream 742

1. Work the stems, leaves and bud 'greenery' in straight stitches.
2. Form the flower by working three rounds of blanket stitch. First work the outer round in dark yellow then the second round in yellow and the inner round in cream.
3. Work the bud in a yellow lazy daisy with two straight stitches in the centre.

13. Tulip

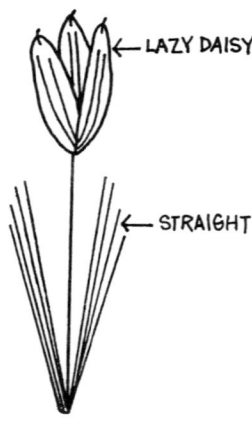

Stem and Leaves
RoyalStitch: green EW50

Flower
Gumnut: light orange 785

1. Work the stem in a straight stitch.
2. Form the flower with three long lazy daisies. Work two straight stitches in the centre of each lazy daisy.
3. Form the leaves with four straight stitches worked closely together.

14. Iris

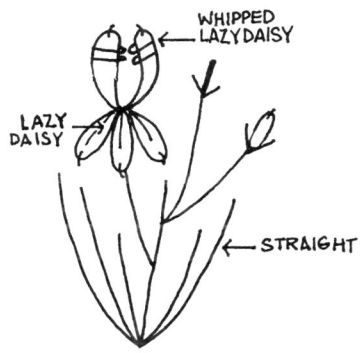

Stems and Leaves
Gumnut: green 586

Flower and Buds
Gumnut: purple 257; light lilac 255

1. Work the stems, leaves and bud 'greenery' in straight stitches.
2. Form the two top petals by working two, light lilac lazy daisies. Whip each lazy daisy.
3. Form the three bottom petals with purple lazy daisies with straight stitch centres.
4. Form the larger bud with a purple lazy daisy, the smaller bud with one, purple straight stitch.

15. Narcissus

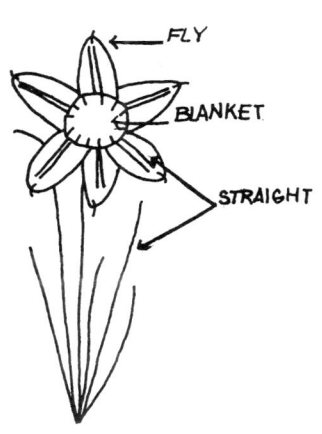

Stem and Leaves
RoyalStitch: green EW50

Flower
RoyalStitch: dark yellow EW70
Gumnut: cream 742

1. Work the stem and leaves in straight stitches.
2. Form the petals with 'wide', cream fly stitches filled in with straight stitches.
3. Work the dark yellow trumpet in a circle of blanket stitch.

DMC Medici	Gumnut	Paterna	RoyalStitch	Appletons Crewel	DMC Tapestry	Anchor Tapestry	Appletons Tapestry
8332	**255**	334	NC	884	7241	8584	884
8333	**257**	332	NC	102	7711	8590	102
8896	**273**	302	EW33	452	7896	8524	452
8413	**586**	613	NC	425	7384	9016	425
8342	**615**	692	NC	543	7771	9096	543
8326	**726**	703	EW70	472	7504	8134	472
8328	**742**	756	NC	841	7905	8052	841
8941	**785**	802	NC	862	7917	8154	862
8415	541	D501	**EW50**	832	7956	8966	832
8026	745	727	**EW70**	741	7055	8058	741

Spring Bulbs

16. Forget-Me-Not

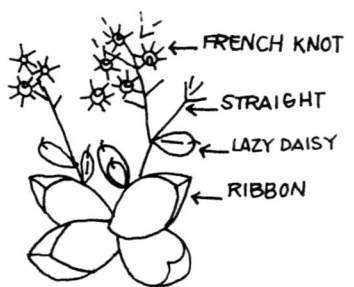

Stems and Leaves
DMC Medici: green 8344
YLI silk ribbon: 7 mm green 20

Flowers and Buds
DMC Medici: blue 8798; pink 8224; yellow 8026

1. Work the stems in straight stitch.
2. Using two strands of blue wool work a straight stitch for each petal. Work another blue straight stitch over the top of each petal using one strand of wool.
3. Work a yellow, single-twist French knot in the centre of each flower.
4. Work the side-view flowers in blue straight stitches.
5. Form the buds with either blue or pink straight stitches.
6. Form the smaller leaves with either a double lazy daisy or a lazy daisy with a straight stitch centre. Work the larger leaves in ribbon stitch with silk ribbon.

17. Calla Lily

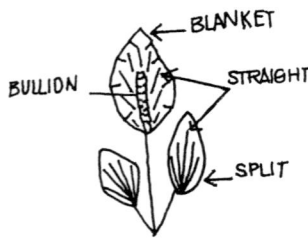

Stem and Leaves
DMC Medici: green 8346

Flower
DMC Medici: yellow 8026; gold 8303A

1. Work the stem in a straight stitch.
2. Form the flower with a yellow 'fan' shape of blanket stitch filled in with straight stitches.
3. Work the stamen in a gold, twelve-wrap bullion.
4. Outline the leaves in split stitch and then fill in with straight stitches.

18. Violet

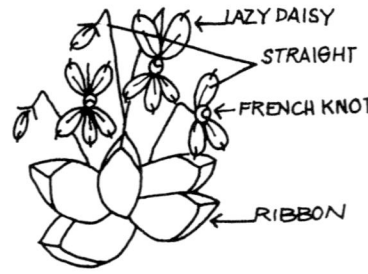

Stems and Leaves
DMC Medici: green 8413
YLI silk ribbon: 7 mm green 20

Flowers and Buds
DMC Medici: purple 8794; dark yellow 8725

1. Work the stems and bud 'greenery' in straight stitches.
2. Form each petal and bud with a purple lazy daisy with a straight stitch centre.
3. Work the centre of each flower in a dark yellow double-twist French knot.
4. Work the leaves in ribbon stitch with silk ribbon.

19. Snapdragon

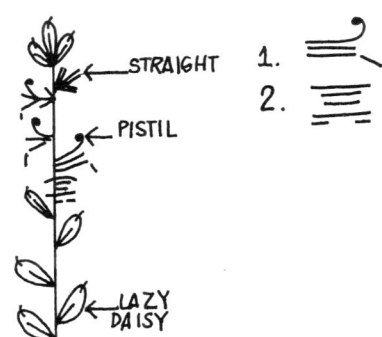

Stem and Leaves
DMC Medici: green 8344

Flowers and Buds
DMC Medici: deep pink 8103

1. Work the stem in a straight stitch.
2. Use pistil stitch and straight stitch to form the flowers. (See diagrams 1 and 2 for detail.)
3. Work the deep pink buds and bud 'greenery' in straight stitches.
4. Work the green buds and leaves in lazy daisies with straight stitch centres.

20. English Daisy

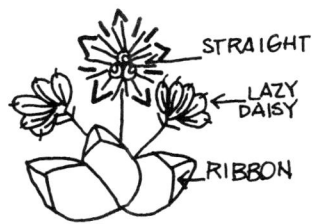

Stems and Leaves
DMC Medici: green 8414
YLI silk ribbon: 7 mm green 32

Flowers
DMC Medici: white; hot pink 8155

1. Work the stems in stem stitch.
2. Work the full-view flower in straight stitches using the white first and then adding the 'flush' of hot pink.
3. Form the side-view flowers by working hot pink lazy daisies with white straight stitch centres. Form the base with small, green straight stitches.
4. Work the leaves in ribbon stitch with silk ribbon.

DMC Medici	Gumnut	Paterna	RoyalStitch	Appletons Crewel	DMC Tapestry	Anchor Tapestry	Appletons Tapestry
white	990	261	NC	991B	white	8004	991B
8026	708	712	EW70	553	7726	8118	553
8103	039	971	NC	503	7849	8202	503
8155	058	350	NC	803	7157	8490	803
8224	863	874	NC	221	7164	9508	221
8303A	C4	702	NC	726	7473	9524	726
8344	608	691	NC	545	7045	9100	545
8346	616	692	NC	544	7769	9102	544
8413	606	D522	NC	831	7542	9004	831
8414	B5	661	NC	833	7540	9022	833
8725	708	613	NC	554	7742	8120	554
8794	277	300	NC	456	7708	8528	456
8798	386	544	EW40	462	7798	8688	462

21. Aquilegia

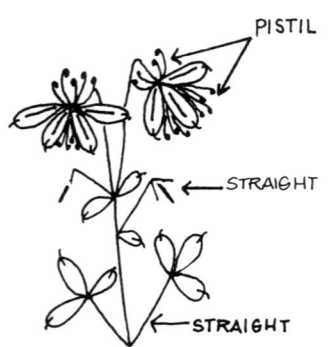

Stems and Leaves
DMC Medici: green 8407

Flowers and Buds
DMC Medici: deep pink 8103;
yellow 8748

1. Work the stems in straight stitch.
2. Work the middle petals in deep pink lazy daisies with straight stitch centres.
3. Work the top petals in deep pink pistil stitch.
4. Work the bottom section of the flower in yellow pistil stitch.
5. Work the buds in a green or deep pink straight stitch.
6. Work the leaves in lazy daisies.

22. Gentian

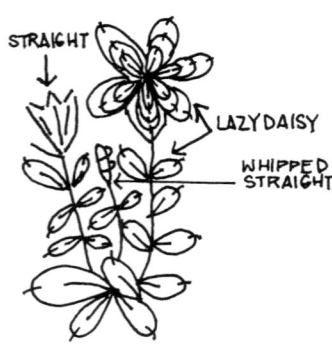

Stems and Leaves
Gumnut: green 587

Flowers and Buds
DMC Medici: navy 8720;
cobalt 8993;
yellow 8026

1. Work the stems in straight stitch.
2. Form the petals with three, cobalt lazy daisies inside each other, with a straight stitch in the inner one.
3. Work the base of the flower in navy straight stitches.
4. Work the stamens in yellow straight stitches
5. Outline the partly open bud in cobalt straight stitches and fill in with cobalt and navy straight stitches.
6. Form the small bud with a cobalt lazy daisy whipped in navy.
7. Work the leaves in lazy daisies with straight stitch centres.

23. Primula

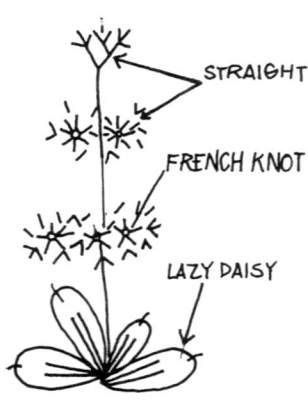

Stem and Leaves
DMC Medici: green 8344

Flowers
Gumnut: pink 055
DMC Medici: yellow 8748

1. Work the stem and bud 'greenery' in straight stitches.
2. Form the flowers with pink straight stitches. Full-view flowers have six, small straight stitches and side-view flowers can have one, two or three straight stitches.
3. Work a yellow, single-twist French knot in the centre of each full flower.
4. Work the leaves in lazy daisies filled in with straight stitches.

24. Sweet Pea

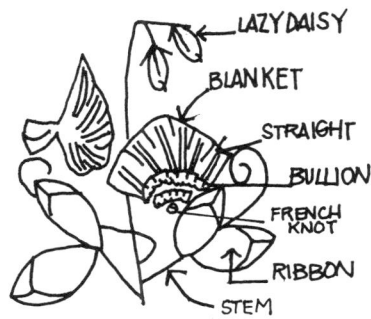

Stems and Leaves
DMC Medici: green 8406
YLI silk ribbon: 7 mm green 33

Flowers and Buds
Gumnut: melon 806

1. Work the stems, trailings and bud 'greenery' in either stem stitch or straight stitch.
2. Form the front-view flower with a semi-circle of blanket stitch filled in with straight stitches. At the base of the blanket stitch work a twelve-wrap bullion chain then a six-wrap bullion chain. Complete the flower with a double-twist French knot.
3. Work the side-view flower in blanket stitch filled in with straight stitches.
4. Work the buds in lazy daisies with straight stitch centres.
5. Work the leaves in ribbon stitch with silk ribbon.

25. Pansy

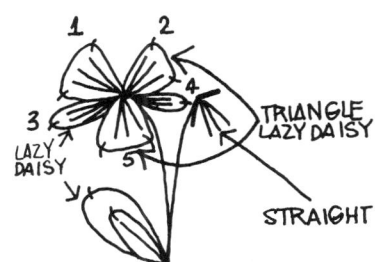

Stems and Leaf
Gumnut: green 567

Flower and Bud
Gumnut: purple 257; yellow 708; light lilac 255
DMC stranded cotton: purple 550; yellow 725

1. Work the stems in straight stitch.
2. Work petals 1 and 2 (purple) and 5 (yellow) in triangle lazy daisies filled in with straight stitches. Work petals 3 and 4 (light lilac) in lazy daisies filled in with straight stitches.
3. Work the 'face' of the flower in straight stitches with three strands of purple cotton and then work a double-twist French knot in the centre with six strands of yellow cotton.
4. Form the leaf by working a double lazy daisy with a straight stitch centre.

DMC Medici	Gumnut	Paterna	RoyalStitch	Appletons Crewel	DMC Tapestry	Anchor Tapestry	Appletons Tapestry
8026	745	712	EW70	553	7726	8058	553
8103	039	971	NC	503	7849	8202	503
8344	608	691	NC	545	7045	9100	545
8406	586	602	NC	832	7370	9078	832
8407	B5	D546	NC	643	7406	9080	643
8720	389	540	NC	465	7796	8692	465
8748	706	714	NC	551	7078	8014	551
8993	408	581	NC	486	7995	8808	486
8816	**055**	903	NC	754	7804	8456	754
8332	**255**	334	NC	884	7241	8584	884
8333	**257**	332	NC	102	7711	8590	102
8406	**567**	662	NC	833	7386	9004	833
8414	**587**	612	NC	428	7320	9018	428
8742	**806**	824	EW13	622	7762	8256	622
8026	**708**	726	NC	471	7725	8118	471

COTTAGE GARDEN FLOWERS 25

26. Dianthus

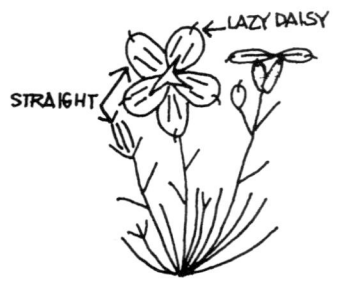

Stems and Leaves
DMC Medici: green 8406

Flower and Buds
Gumnut: pink 054
DMC Medici: white

1. Work the stems, leaves and bud 'greenery' in straight stitches.
2. Work the flower in pink lazy daisies filled in with straight stitches.
3. Work the stamen in white straight stitches.
4. Form the bud with pink straight stitches.
5. Work the side-view flower in two lazy daisies with straight stitch centres.

27. Lilium

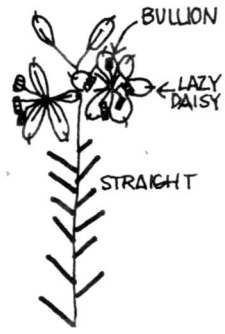

Stem and Leaves
DMC Medici: dark green 8403

Flowers and Buds
DMC Medici: orange 8908
DMC stranded cotton: 3371

1. Work the stem and leaves in straight stitches using two strands of wool.
2. Work the petals and buds in lazy daisies with straight stitch centres.
3. Using one strand of stranded cotton form the stamens by working a straight stitch at the end of which is worked a six-wrap bullion.

28. Geranium

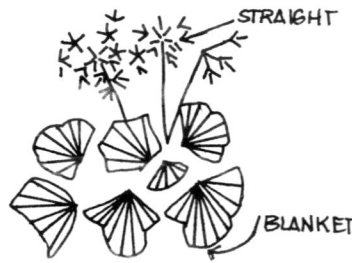

Stems and Leaves
DMC Medici: green 8344

Flowers and Buds
Gumnut: red 039

1. Work the stems in straight stitch.
2. Work the flowers, buds and bud 'greenery' in straight stitches.
3. Form the leaves with an outline of uneven blanket stitch filled in with straight stitches.

29. Primrose

Stems and Leaves
DMC Medici: tan 8308;
    green 8346

Flower and Buds
DMC Medici: yellow 8027;
    soft green 8420

1. Work the stems in tan split stitch.
2. Form each petal by working two, yellow, uneven fly stitches filled in with straight stitches. Work the soft green centre in five straight stitches and a double-twist French knot.
3. Work the leaves in stacked fly stitch.
4. Form the buds with lazy daisies with straight stitch centres. Work the bases in soft green straight stitches.

30. MORNING GLORY

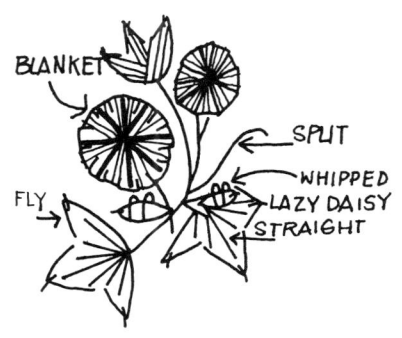

Stems and Leaves
DMC Medici: light green 8369

Flowers and Buds
DMC Medici: blue 8899; navy 8720;
light dusky pink 8210A

1. Work the stems in split stitch.
2. Work the flower in a circle of ten, blue blanket stitches filled in with straight stitches.
3. Work five, navy straight stitches and then five, light dusky pink straight stitches to complete the flower.
4. Form the buds with blue lazy daisies whipped in light dusky pink.
5. Form the outline of the leaves in even and uneven fly stitch. Fill in with straight stitches.

31. SCABIOUS

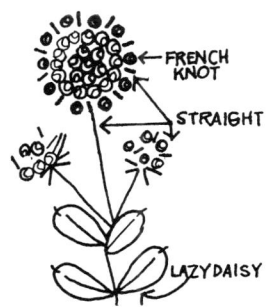

Stems and Leaves
Gumnut: green 566

Flower and Buds
Gumnut: dark mauve 299;
light mauve 297;
light green C3

1. Work the stems and bud 'greenery' in straight stitches.
2. Form the centre of the flower with a single-twist French knot surrounded by a circle of single-twist French knots using dark mauve.
3. With light mauve work another round of single-twist French knots. Form the final round by alternating single-twist French knots and straight stitches.
4. Work the buds in five, light green French knots and three straight stitches.
5. Work the leaves in lazy daisies with straight stitch centres.

DMC Medici	Gumnut	Paterna	RoyalStitch	Appletons Crewel	DMC Tapestry	Anchor Tapestry	Appletons Tapestry
white	990	261	NC	991B	white	8004	991B
8027	708	713	NC	552	7727	8114	552
8120A	966	D133	NC	220	7949	9618	220
8308	645	643	NC	952	7413	9326	952
8344	608	691	NC	545	7045	9100	545
8346	616	692	NC	544	7769	9102	544
8369	604	605	NC	401	7402	9014	401
8403	608	691	NC	256	7320	9206	256
8406	586	602	NC	832	7370	9078	832
8420	675	635	NC	251A	7340	9194	251A
8720	389	540	NC	465	7796	8692	465
8899	389	543	EW40	303	7316	8688	303
8908	809	810	NC	626	7947	8168	626
8400	C3	653	EW60	693	7422	9304	693
8103	039	971	NC	503	7849	8202	503
8151	054	904	NC	753	7151	8454	753
8333	299	332	NC	895	7241	8590	895
8406	566	664	NC	832	7370	9002	832
8332	297	333	NC	894	7244	8588	894

32. Evening Primrose

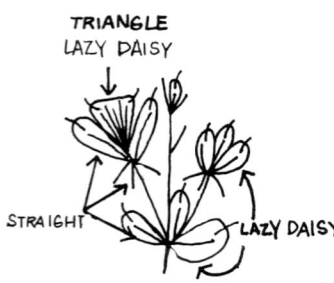

Stems and Leaves
Gumnut: light green C3; green 567

Flowers and Buds
Gumnut: lemon 744

1. Work the stems in light green straight stitch.
2. Form the middle petal with a triangle lazy daisy filled in with straight stitches.
3. Work the two side petals and buds in lazy daisies with straight stitch centres.
4. Work the leaves in green lazy daisies with straight stitch centres.

33. Cyclamen

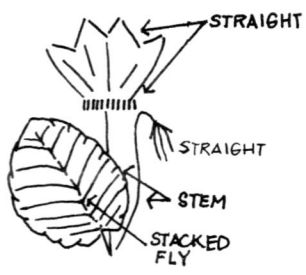

Stems and Leaf
DMC Medici: brown 8108; green 8413

Flower and Bud
DMC Medici: bright pink 8153; light pink 8151

1. Work the stem and bud 'greenery' in brown straight stitches.
2. Outline the petals in bright pink straight stitches. Fill in with a mixture of the pinks using straight stitches.
3. Complete the flower by working a row of short, bright pink straight stitches.
4. Work the bud in three, bright pink straight stitches.
5. Work the leaf in green stacked fly stitch.

34. Viola

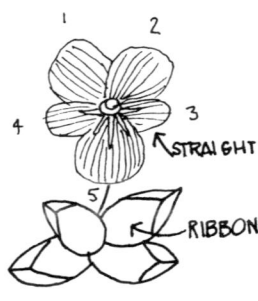

Stems and Leaves
Gumnut: green 616
YLI silk ribbon: 7 mm green 20

Flower and Bud
RoyalStitch: purple EW30; yellow EW77; dark yellow EW70

1. Work the stems, flower, bud and bud 'greenery' in straight stitches.
2. Form petals 1 and 2 with seven purple stitches, petals 3 and 4 with five yellow stitches and petal 5 with thirteen dark yellow stitches.
3. Work the 'face' of the flower in purple straight stitches and a dark yellow French knot.
4. Work the leaves in ribbon stitch with silk ribbon.

35. Fritillary

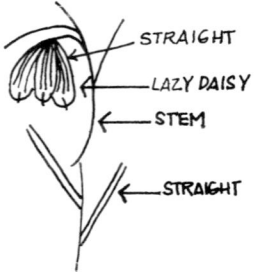

Stem and Leaves
Gumnut: green 587

Flower
Gumnut: pink R5

1. Work the stem in stem stitch.
2. Work the petals in lazy daisies filling in each with three straight stitches.
3. Work the bottom leaves in two straight stitches worked closely together. Form the top leaves with a single straight stitch.

36. COTTON WEED

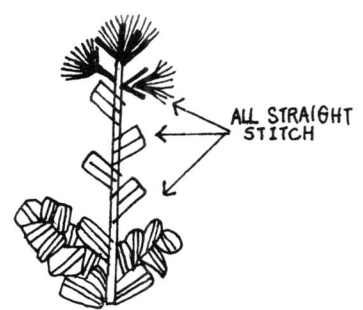

Stem and Leaves
Anchor tapestry wool: gray 9782

Flowers
DMC Medici: dark yellow 8725

1. Work the stem, flowers and leaves in straight stitches.
2. Work the stem and the base of the flowers first then the dark yellow petals. Add the leaves last.

37. HEATHER

Stem and Leaves
DMC Medici: green 8407

Buds and Flowers
DMC Medici: pink 8817

1. Work the stem, buds, bud 'greenery' and leaves in straight stitches.
2. Work the flowers in straight stitches as shown in the diagram.

DMC Medici	Gumnut	Paterna	RoyalStitch	Appletons Crewel	DMC Tapestry	Anchor Tapestry	Appletons Tapestry
8108	907	403	NC	124	7063	9512	124
8151	054	904	NC	753	7151	8454	753
8153	196	353	NC	801	7153	8488	801
8407	B5	D546	NC	643	7406	9080	643
8413	606	D522	NC	831	7542	9004	831
8725	360	613	EW70	554	7742	8120	554
8817	039	960	NC	946	7136	8438	946
8405	**C3**	653	EW60	693	7422	9304	693
8223	**R5**	913	NC	145	7153	8420	145
8406	**567**	662	NC	833	7386	9004	833
8414	**587**	612	NC	428	7320	9018	428
8419	**616**	693	NC	544	7769	9100	544
8748	**744**	743	EW73	743	7579	8056	842
8794	277	300	**EW30**	456	7708	8528	456
8026	745	727	**EW70**	473	7055	8058	473
8748	744	704	**EW77**	471	7745	8056	471
8381	292	256	NC	876	7067	**9782**	876

38. Petunia

Stems and Leaves
RoyalStitch: green EW50;
    sand EW63

Flowers and Bud
RoyalStitch: purple EW30;
    variegated purple EW37

1. Work the stems in green straight stitch.
2. Work the centre of each flower in three, purple, horizontal straight stitches. With two strands of variegated purple wool work the petals in straight stitches.
3. Complete the flower by working the base in purple straight stitches.
4. Work the head of the bud in purple straight stitches. Work the base in sand straight stitches.
5. Work the leaves in lazy daisies with straight stitch centres.

39. Wallflower

Stems and Leaves
DMC Medici: green 8344

Flower and Buds
DMC Medici: red 8127; rust 8104

1. Work the stems and bud 'greenery' in straight stitches.
2. To work the flower have a strand of red and rust wool in the needle.
3. Form the centre of the flower with four, short straight stitches. At the end of these stitches work a lazy daisy filled with two straight stitches.
4. Work the buds and leaves in lazy daisies with straight stitch centres.

40. Clematis

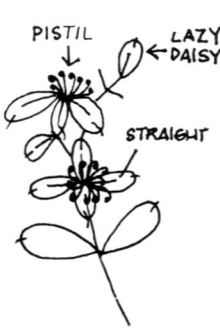

Stem and Leaves
Gumnut: green 586

Flowers and Bud
Gumnut: cream 742
DMC stranded cotton: lemon 745

1. Work the stem in a straight stitch.
2. Work the petals in cream lazy daisies with straight stitch centres.
3. Work the stamens in pistil stitch using two strands of lemon cotton.
4. Work the bud in a lazy daisy with a straight stitch centre.
5. Work the leaves in lazy daisy.

41. Thistle

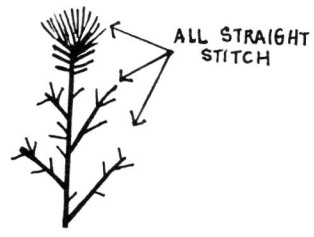

Stems and Thorns
DMC Medici: dark green 8415;

Flower
DMC Medici: raspberry 8101
yellow green 8420

1. With one strand of dark green and yellow green in the needle together work the stems and base of the flowerhead in straight stitches.
2. Work the top of the flower in raspberry straight stitches.
3. Work the thorns in small, dark green straight stitches.

42. Dahlia

Stems and Leaves
Gumnut: green 566; brown 867
YLI silk ribbon: 7 mm green 33

Flower and Buds
Gumnut: orange 766

1. Work the stems in brown straight stitch.
2. Form the flower with three rounds of straight stitches. The outer round has the longer stitches.
3. Work the buds and bud 'greenery' in straight stitches.
4. Work the leaves in ribbon stitch with silk ribbon.

DMC Medici	Gumnut	Paterna	RoyalStitch	Appletons Crewel	DMC Tapestry	Anchor Tapestry	Appletons Tapestry
8101	097	901	NC	758	7138	8458	758
8104	H5	720	NC	207	7446	9560	207
8127	857	970	NC	504	7666	8200	504
8344	608	691	NC	545	7045	9100	545
8415	D5	D516	NC	646	7701	8884	646
8420	675	635	NC	251A	7340	9194	251A
8406	**566**	664	NC	832	7370	9002	832
8413	**586**	613	NC	425	7384	9016	425
8328	**742**	756	NC	841	7905	8052	841
8026	**745**	727	EW70	741	7503	8058	741
8742	**766**	814	NC	861	7742	8152	861
8941	**785**	802	NC	862	7917	8154	862
8108	**867**	472	NC	205	7165	9620	205
8509	TP2	654	**EW63**	971	7331	9052	971
8794	277	300	**EW30**	456	7708	8528	456
8415	541	D501	**EW50**	832	7956	8966	832
8896	275	302	**EW37**	453	7895	8588	453

43. GLADIOLI

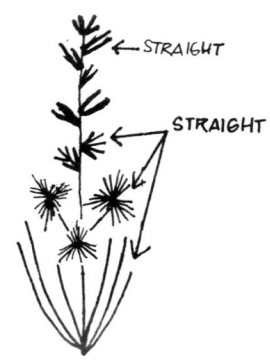

Stem and Leaves
Gumnut: green 616

Flowers and Buds
Gumnut: red 038

1. Work the stem in a straight stitch.
2. Work the flowers (see diagram) and buds in straight stitches.
3. Work the leaves in straight stitches.

44. DANDELION

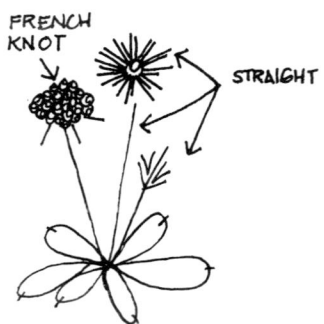

Stems, Bud and Leaves
Gumnut: green 587

Flower and Seedhead
Gumnut: yellow 708
DMC Medici: white

1. Work the stems, bud and seedhead 'greenery' in straight stitches.
2. Form the centre with a yellow, single-twist French knot and each petal with two, yellow straight stitches worked closely together.
3. Form the seedhead with white, single-twist French knots.
4. Work the leaves in lazy daisies.

45. HYDRANGEA

Stems and Leaves
YLI silk ribbon:
4 mm bright green 61

Flowers
RoyalStitch: mid-blue EW40;
variegated blue EW43

1. Work the stems in straight stitch with silk ribbon.
2. With one strand of each blue together form the flowers with single-twist French knots.
3. Work the leaves in ribbon stitch with silk ribbon.

46. HOLLYHOCK

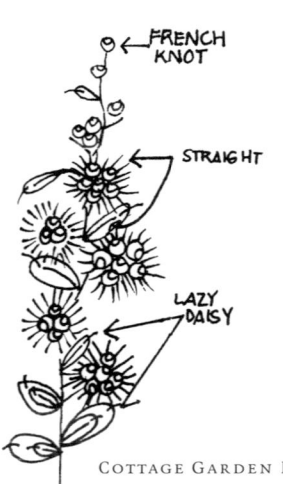

Stem and Leaves
DMC Perle cotton 8: green 367

Flowers and Buds
RoyalStitch: variegated pink EW27

1. Work the stem in a straight stitch.
2. Work the buds in a double-twist French knot.
3. Form the centre of the flowers with single-twist French knots using two stands of wool. Surround the centre with straight stitches.
4. Work the leaves with either a double lazy daisy or a single lazy daisy with a straight stitch centre.

COTTAGE GARDEN FLOWERS

47. Delphinium

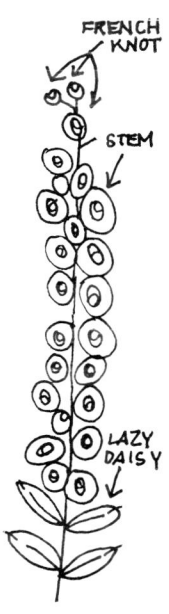

Stem, Buds and Leaves
DMC Perle cotton 8: green 367

Flowers
Appletons crewel wool: cobalt 485 & 486; navy 928

1. Work the stem in a straight stitch.
2. With two strands of navy work a single-twist French knot to form the centre of each floweret.
3. With a strand of each shade of cobalt work one round of stem stitch around the French knot centre.
4. Form the buds with a green, four-twist French knot.
5. Form the leaves with a lazy daisy with a straight stitch centre.

48. Foxglove

Stems and Leaves
DMC Perle cotton 8: green 367

Flowers and Buds
Appletons crewel wool: pink 945; burgundy 948

1. Work the stems in straight stitch.
2. Work the green and pink buds in small straight stitches.
3. Work the partly opened flowerets at the top of the plant in small, pink lazy daisies.
4. Work the fully opened flowerets in larger, pink lazy daisies with burgundy straight stitch centres.
5. Work the leaves in lazy daisy.

DMC Medici	Gumnut	Paterna	RoyalStitch	Appletons Crewel	DMC Tapestry	Anchor Tapestry	Appletons Tapestry
white	990	260	NC	991B	white	8004	991B
8666	**038**	970	NC	502	7666	8200	502
8026	**708**	771	NC	551	7973	8118	551
8414	**587**	612	NC	428	7320	9018	428
8419	**616**	693	NC	544	7769	9100	544
8151	153	913	**EW27**	754	7133	8414	754
8899	387	544	**EW40**	463	7314	8688	463
8799	364	546	**EW43**	461	7800	8682	461
8995	428	590	NC	**485**	7037	8806	485
8993	408	582	NC	**486**	7038	8808	486
8200	O5	510	NC	**928**	7590	8744	928
8817	019	903	NC	**945**	7135	8438	945
8101	157	902	NC	**948**	7138	8402	948

49. Queen Anne's Lace

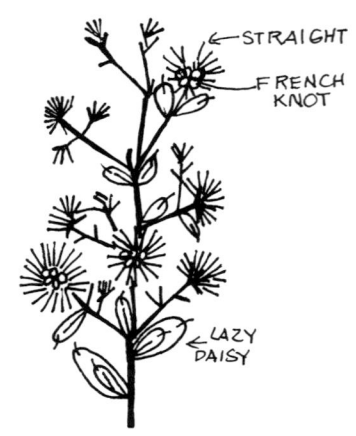

Stems and Leaves
DMC Perle cotton 8: green 367

Flowers
DMC Medici: white

1. Work the flowers in a mixture of single- and double-twist French knots.
2. Work the stems and leaves in straight stitches.

50. Michaelmas Daisy

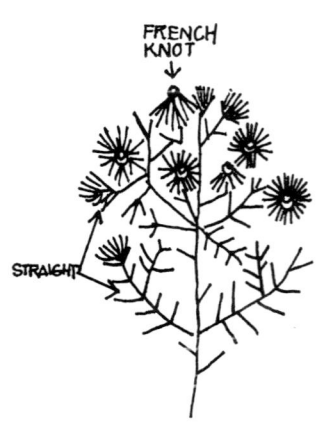

Stems and Leaves
Gumnut: brown 987
DMC Medici: green 8402

Flowers and Buds
Paterna: mauve 343
RoyalStitch: dark yellow EW70

1. Work the main stem and 'side' stems in brown straight stitches.
2. Work the full flowers in mauve straight stitches. Complete the flower by working five, dark yellow, single-twist French knots.
3. Work the side-view flowers and buds in mauve straight stitches.
4. Add 'greenery', small leaves and stems to the buds in short, green straight stitches.
5. Work the leaves in either a single or double green lazy daisy.

51. Ragwort

Stems and Leaves
Appletons crewel wool: green 254

Flowers and Buds
RoyalStitch: dark yellow EW70
DMC Medici: gold 8303A

1. Work the stems in straight stitch.
2. Work the full-view flowers in dark yellow straight stitches. Complete the flower with three, gold, single-twist French knots.
3. Work the buds and side-view flowers in dark yellow straight stitches.
4. Work the leaves and bud 'greenery' in straight stitches.

34 COTTAGE GARDEN FLOWERS

52. Astilbe

Stem and Leaves
DMC Perle cotton 8: green 367
YLI silk ribbon 7 mm: green 20

Flower
Appletons crewel wool: red 445

1. Work the stem in a straight stitch.
2. Work straight stitches for the very small flowerets at the top of the stem then work two, six-wrap bullions increasing the wraps to eight, ten and twelve as you work down the stem.
3. Work the leaves in ribbon stitch with silk ribbon.

53. Agapanthus

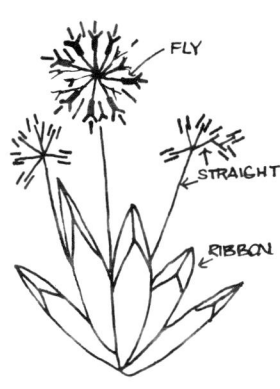

Stems and Leaves
DMC Perle cotton 8: green 367
YLI silk ribbon 4 mm: green 32

Flowers and Buds
Paterna: periwinkle 342
DMC Perle cotton 8: green 367

1. Work the main stem in a straight stitch and add eight straight stitches to form the foundation of the flower.
2. Work a fly stitch at the end of each of the eight prongs then add another small straight stitch to the centre of each fly stitch.
3. Work the buds on the main flower and semi-open flower in periwinkle straight stitches.
4. Form the green buds with three, small straight stitches at the end of a straight stitch.
5. Work the leaves in long ribbon stitch with silk ribbon.

DMC Medici	Gumnut	Paterna	RoyalStitch	Appletons Crewel	DMC Tapestry	Anchor Tapestry	Appletons Tapestry
white	990	260	NC	991B	white	8004	991B
8402	608	651	NC	255	7364	9200	255
8303A	C5	702	NC	726	7473	8020	726
8125	**987**	D115	NC	584	7416	8512	584
8332	297	**342**	NC	894	7020	8608	894
8331	295	**343**	NC	893	7019	8606	893
8026	745	727	EW70	741	7055	8058	741
8402	607	692	NC	**254**	7364	9168	254
8666	827	820	NC	**445**	7606	8198	445

54. Lythrum

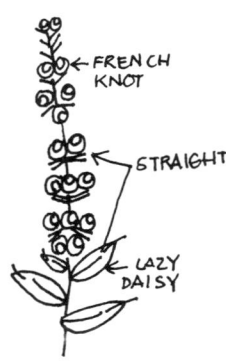

Stem and Leaves
DMC Perle cotton 8: green 367
Gumnut: green 587

Flowers and Buds
Gumnut: pink 076
DMC Perle cotton 8: green 367

1. Work the stem in a straight stitch.
2. With two strands of pink work the flowerets in a single-twist French knot.
3. With green, work the small buds in a double-twist French knot, small leaves in straight stitch and larger leaves in a lazy daisy with a straight stitch centre.

55. Tiger Lily (Turk's Cap)

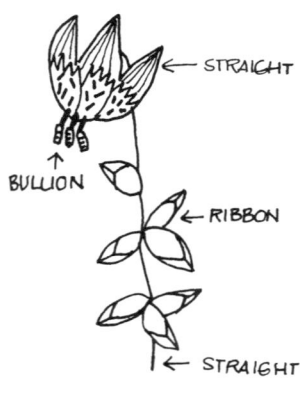

Stem and Leaves
DMC Perle cotton 8: green 367
YLI silk ribbon 4 mm:
    deep green 75

Flower
Appletons crewel wool: rich yellow 555;
    rust 866
DMC stranded cotton: dark brown 3371;
    burgundy 902

1. Work the stem in a straight stitch.
2. Form the flower by outlining the shape of the top of the petals in rust straight stitches.
3. Fill in with straight stitches.
4. Outline the base of the petals in rich yellow and fill in with long and short straight stitches.
5. Randomly work very small straight stitches with two strands of dark brown cotton over the rich yellow.
6. Form the stamens by working three, green straight stitches. At the end of each straight stitch work a six-wrap bullion with two strands of burgundy.
7. Work the leaves in ribbon stitch with silk ribbon.

56. Alkanet

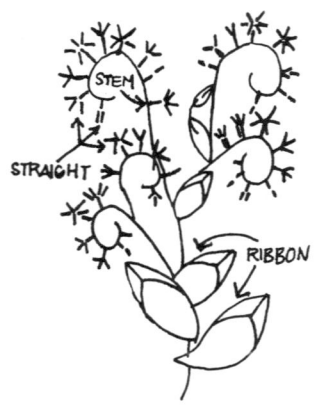

Stems and Leaves
DMC stranded cotton: green 3347
YLI silk ribbon 7 mm: green 20

Flowers and Buds
Appletons crewel wool: blue 746;
    purple 455;
    light fuchsia 801;
    fuchsia 803

1. Using two strands of stranded cotton work the stems in stem stitch and then work the base of each flower in two small straight stitches.
2. Using two strands of wool and mixing the colours, work the full-view flowers, side-view flowers and buds in small straight stitches.
3. Work the leaves in ribbon stitch with silk ribbon.

57. LUPIN

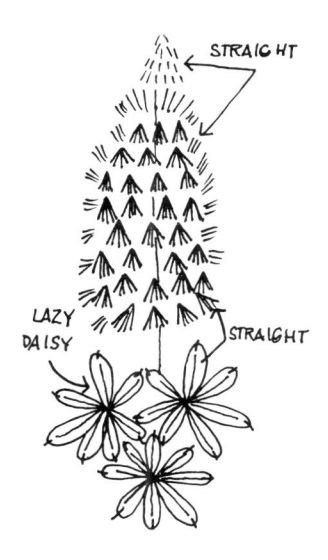

Stem and Leaves
DMC Perle cotton 8: green 367

Flower
RoyalStitch: dark yellow EW70;
purple EW30
DMC Perle cotton 8: green 367

1. Work the stem and small buds at the top of the plant in green straight stitches.
2. Work all the flowerets in small straight stitches.
3. Work the side of the plant in clusters of three very close, purple stitches.
4. Work the flowerets in the main part of the plant in dark yellow and purple.
5. First work a very small ⋀ in dark yellow with two stitches, then work three purple stitches into this 'cap'.
6. Build the rows as you work, i.e. work a row of dark yellow, fill in with purple, then move down to the next row and repeat.
7. Work the leaves in long lazy daisies with straight stitch centres.

58. JAPANESE ANEMONE

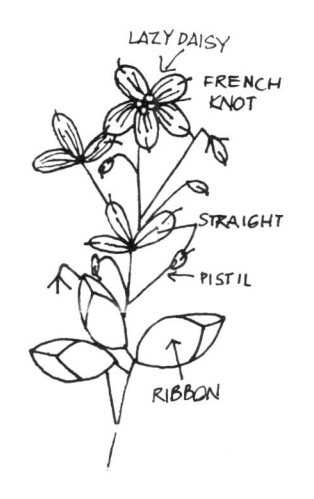

Stems and Leaves
DMC Perle cotton 8: green 367
YLI silk ribbon 7 mm: green 33

Flowers and Buds
DMC Medici: dark pink 8685;
gold 8303A

1. Work the five petals in large, dark pink 'plump' lazy daisies, then fill in each with three straight stitches. Complete the flower with four, gold, single-twist French knots.
2. Form the side-view flower with three, filled-in 'plump' lazy daisies.
3. Work the stems in straight stitch.
4. Form the buds with either straight stitches with bud 'greenery' or a pistil stitch with a small, dark pink straight stitch stitched into the knot.
5. Work the flower in ribbon stitch with silk ribbon and the upper leaves in a lazy daisy with a straight stitch centre using Perle cotton.

DMC Medici	Gumnut	Paterna	RoyalStitch	Appletons Crewel	DMC Tapestry	Anchor Tapestry	Appletons Tapestry
8685	077	903	NC	803	7600	8458	803
8303A	C5	702	NC	726	7473	8020	726
8155	**076**	904	NC	145	7603	8456	145
8414	**587**	612	NC	428	7320	9018	428
8794	277	300	**EW30**	456	7708	8528	456
8026	745	727	**EW70**	741	7055	8058	741
8794	277	300	NC	**455**	7017	8528	455
8325	708	771	NC	**555**	7056	8122	555
8207	348	560	NC	**746**	7033	8630	746
8153	215	352	NC	**801**	7153	8490	801
8685	197	350	NC	**803**	7157	8492	803
8104	887	850	NC	**866**	7920	8236	866

59. JAPANESE IRIS

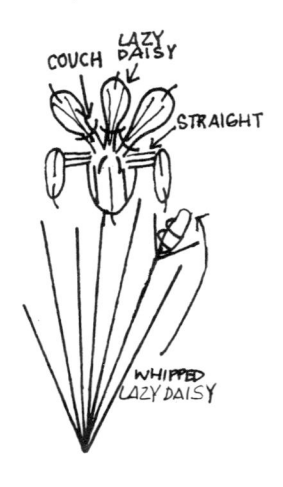

Stems and Leaves
Gumnut: green 541

Flower and Bud
Gumnut: dark purple 277; lilac 233

1. Work the three top petals in a dark purple, long lazy daisy and couch 1/3rd from the base of the stitch. Fill in the top with one or two straight stitches.
2. Work the middle, lower petal in a 'plump', lilac lazy daisy and fill in with three straight stitches.
3. Work the side, lower petals in lilac straight stitches and lazy daisies with straight stitch centres.
4. Work the bud in a whipped lazy daisy.
5. Work the stems, leaves and bud 'greenery' in straight stitches.

60. LARKSPUR

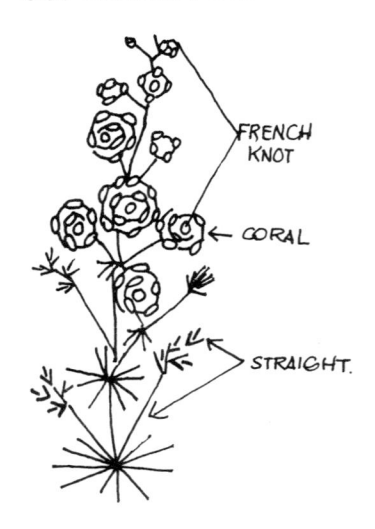

Stems and Leaves
DMC Perle cotton 8: green 367

Flowers and Buds
Gumnut: pink 055
DMC Perle cotton 8: green 367

1. Work the buds at the top of the plant in pink, single- or double-twist French knots.
2. Work the flowers in coral stitch rings. The smaller flowers have one round, the larger and majority of the flowers have two rounds.
3. Complete the flowers by working a green, single-twist French knot in the centre.
4. Work stems, buds, bud 'greenery' and leaves in straight stitches.

DMC Medici	Gumnut	Paterna	Appletons Tapestry	DMC Tapestry	RoyalStitch	Appletons Crewel	Anchor Tapestry
8794	**277**	300	EW30	456	7708	8528	456
8397	**233**	304	NC	884	7790	8522	884
8415	**541**	D501	EW57	832	7956	8966	832
8816	**055**	903	NC	754	7804	8456	754

HERBS

GRASSES

HERBS
61. Thyme
62. Chives
63. Parsley
64. Sage
65. Coriander
66. Pot Marigold
67. Pink Lavender
68. Rosemary
69. Dill
70. Peppermint
71. French Lavender
72. Chamomile
73. Marsh mallow
74. Marjoram
75. Chicory

GRASSES
76. Quaking Grass
77. Barley
78. Clover
79. Rush
80. Wild Oat
81. Fescue
82. Wheat
83. False Foxtail
84. Sharp Rush
85. Meadow Grass
86. Great Millet
87. Cocksfoot

61. Thyme	62. Chives	63. Parsley	64. Sage	65. Coriander
66. Pot Marigold	67. Pink Lavender	68. Rosemary	69. Dill	70. Peppermint
71. French Lavender	72. Chamomile	73. Marsh mallow	74. Marjoram	75. Chicory

76. Quaking Grass	77. Barley	78. Clover	79. Rush
80. Wild Oat	81. Fescue	82. Wheat	83. False Foxtail
84. Sharp Rush	85. Meadow Grass	86. Great Millet	87. Cocksfoot

Herbs

Grasses

61. Thyme

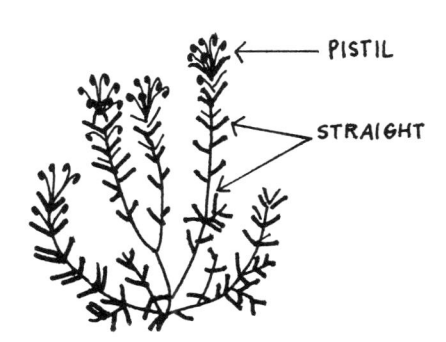

Stems and Leaves
Gumnut: brown 867; green 567

Flowers
Gumnut: pink 116

1. Work the stems in brown straight stitch.
2. Form the flowers by working clumps of pistil stitch.
3. Work the buds in straight stitch.
4. Form the leaves with one or two, green straight stitches.

62. Chives

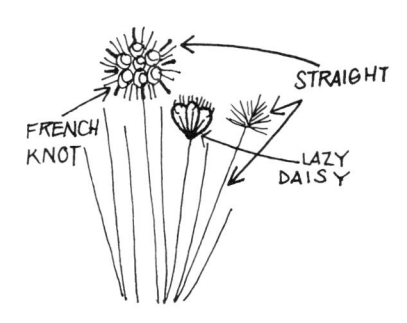

Stems and Leaves
Gumnut: green 587

Flowers and Bud
Gumnut: mauve 235; beige 643

1. Work the stems and leaves in straight stitches.
2. Form the front-view flower by working seven, mauve, single-twist French knots. Complete the flower by working a circle of mauve straight stitches of uneven lengths.
3. Work the side-view flower and bud in mauve straight stitches. Form the base of the bud with beige lazy daisies with straight stitch centres.

63. Parsley

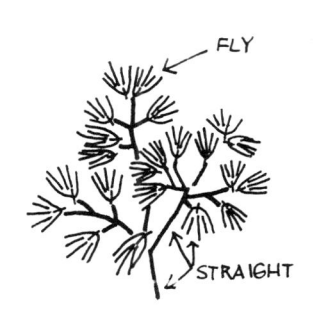

Stems and Leaves
Gumnut: green 616

1. Work the stems in straight stitch.
2. Form the parsley leaves by working a fly stitch and filling it with three straight stitches. Make the centre stitch slightly longer.

DMC Medici	Gumnut	Paterna	RoyalStitch	Appletons Crewel	DMC Tapestry	Anchor Tapestry	Appletons Tapestry
8155	**116**	913	EW20	711	7204	8484	711
8896	**235**	323	EW33	603	7896	8524	603
8406	**567**	662	NC	833	7386	9004	833
8414	**587**	612	NC	428	7320	9018	428
8419	**616**	693	NC	544	7769	9100	544
8421	**643**	644	EW63	331A	7371	9302	331A
8108	**867**	472	NC	205	7165	9620	205

64. Sage

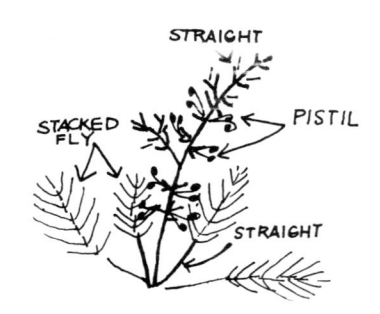

Stem and Leaves
Gumnut: green 566

Flowers and Buds
Gumnut: purple 257

1. Work the stem in a straight stitch.
2. Form the flowers with two pistil stitches.
3. Form the buds and bud 'greenery' with small straight stitches.
4. Work the leaves in stacked fly stitch.

65. Coriander

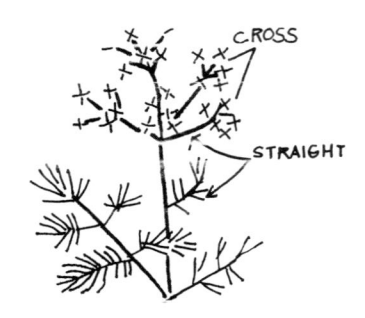

Stems and Leaves
Gumnut: green 567

Flowers
Gumnut: pink 054

1. Work the stems and leaves in straight stitches.
2. Form the flowers with very small cross stitches.

66. Pot Marigold

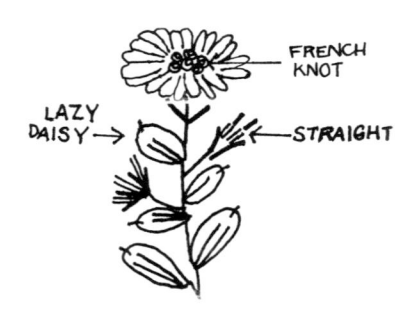

Stem and Leaves
Gumnut: green 616

Flower and Buds
Gumnut: light orange 785; orange 809

1. Work the stem in a straight stitch.
2. Form the petals with straight stitch using two strands of orange wool. Fill in the centre with light orange, single-twist French knots.
3. Work the buds in straight stitches using two strands of orange wool. Complete the bud with green straight stitches.
4. Work the leaves in lazy daisies filled in with straight stitches.

67. Pink Lavender

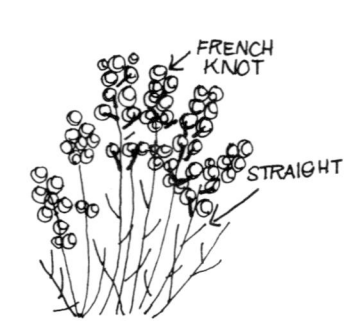

Stems and Leaves
Gumnut: green 566

Flowers
Gumnut: pink 232; beige 643

1. Work the stems and leaves in straight stitches.
2. Form the flowerheads with pink, single-twist French knots. Work small beige straight stitches into some of the French knots.

68. Rosemary

Stems and Leaves
Gumnut: green 567

Flowers
Gumnut: blue 386

1. Work the stems and leaves in straight stitches.
2. Form the flowers with straight stitches.

69. Dill

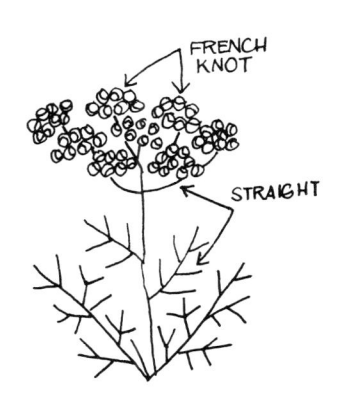

Stem and Leaves
Gumnut: green 615

Flowers
Gumnut: yellow 726

1. Work the stem and leaves in straight stitches.
2. Form the flowers with clusters of single-twist French knots.

DMC Medici	Gumnut	Paterna	RoyalStitch	Appletons Crewel	DMC Tapestry	Anchor Tapestry	Appletons Tapestry
8151	**054**	904	NC	753	7151	8454	753
8118	**232**	325	NC	884	7260	8542	884
8895	**257**	332	NC	895	7711	8590	895
8798	**386**	545	EW43	462	7798	8686	462
8406	**566**	644	NC	832	7370	9002	832
8406	**567**	662	NC	833	7386	9004	833
8342	**615**	692	NC	543	7771	9096	543
8419	**616**	693	NC	544	7769	9100	544
8421	**643**	644	EW63	331A	7371	9302	331A
8326	**726**	703	NC	472	7504	8134	472
8941	**785**	802	NC	862	7917	8154	862
8940	**809**	853	NC	441	7919	8166	441

70. Peppermint

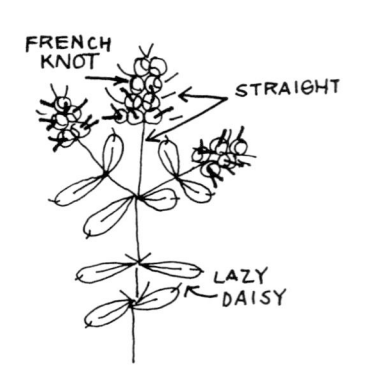

Stems and Leaves
Gumnut: green 587

Flowers
Gumnut: light lilac 255
DMC stranded cotton: pink 3688

1. Work the stems in straight stitch.
2. Form the flowers with single-twist French knots. Work small straight stitches at the top of the flower.
3. With one strand of pink cotton work one or two small straight stitches into the centre of each French knot.
4. Work the leaves in a lazy daisy with a straight stitch centre.

71. French Lavender

Stems and Leaves
Gumnut: green 566

Flowers
RoyalStitch: purple EW30
Appletons crewel wool: navy 106

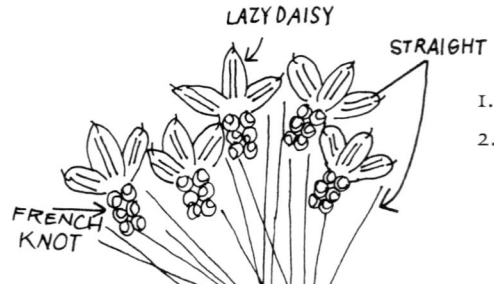

1. Work the stems and leaves in straight stitches.
2. Form the lower part of the flowers with six, navy single-twist French knots. Work the top three petals in purple lazy daisies filled in with straight stitches.

72. Chamomile

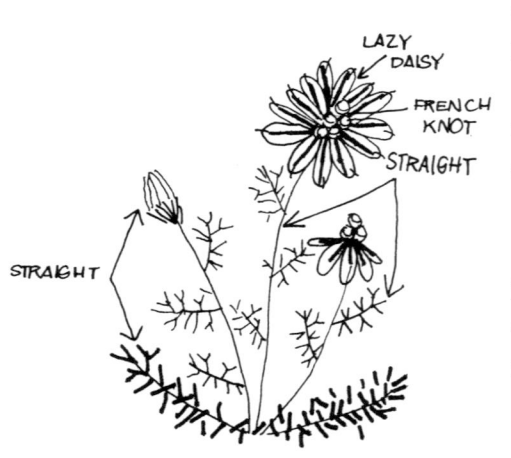

Stem and Leaves
Gumnut: green 587
DMC stranded cotton: green 904

Flowers and Bud
Gumnut: 990; lemon 745
DMC stranded cotton: grey 762

1. Work the stems in straight stitch.
2. Form the centre of the flowers with lemon, single-twist French knots. Work the petals in white straight stitches using two strands of wool. Surround each petal with a lazy daisy using one strand of grey cotton.
3. Work the bud in white straight stitch.
4. Work the bud 'greenery' and larger leaves in green straight stitches.
5. Work the smaller leaves in straight stitch using a single strand of green stranded cotton.

73. MARSH MALLOW

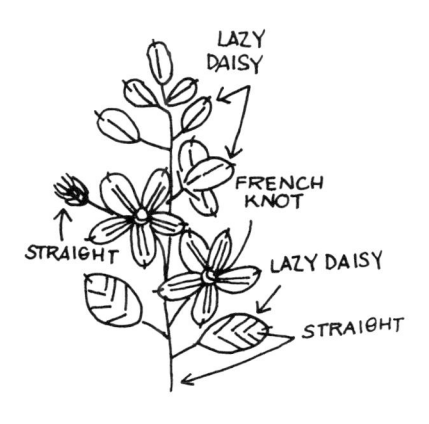

Stems and Leaves
Gumnut: light green 543
pale green 542

Flowers and Buds
Gumnut: dark pink 057; pink 054

1. Work the stems in light green straight stitch.
2. Work the full flowers in five, pink lazy daisies filled in with two straight stitches. Complete the flowers with a dark pink, double-twist French knot in the centre.
3. Work the upper leaves and side-view flower in lazy daisies with straight stitch centres.
4. Work the buds in pink straight stitch.
5. Work the bud 'greenery in pale green straight stitch.
6. Form the lower leaves with a 'plump' lazy daisy filled in with straight stitches worked at right angles to each other.

74. MARJORAM

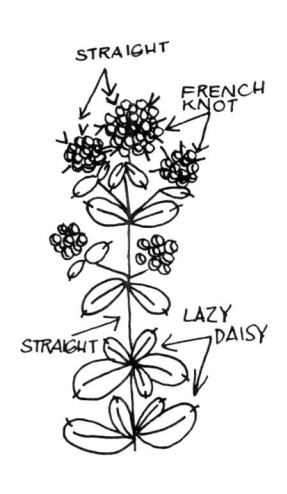

Stems and Leaves
Gumnut: brown 867; green 566

Flowers
Gumnut: deep pink 077; dark pink 057

1. Work the stems in brown straight stitch.
2. Form the centre of the flowers with a deep pink, double-twist French knot. Work two circles of deep pink, double-twist French knots around the centre.
3. Over the top of the French knots work small, light pink straight stitches.
4. Form the leaves and 'greenery' with either lazy daisies or lazy daisies filled in with straight stitches.

DMC Medici	Gumnut	Paterna	RoyalStitch	Appletons Crewel	DMC Tapestry	Anchor Tapestry	Appletons Tapestry
white	**990**	261	NC	991B	white	8004	991B
8151	**054**	904	NC	753	7151	8454	753
8155	**057**	903	NC	755	7602	8456	755
8685	**077**	902	NC	758	7002	8458	758
8332	**255**	334	NC	884	7241	8584	884
8871	**542**	665	NC	522	7040	8982	522
8369	**543**	664	NC	523	7604	8984	523
8406	**566**	644	NC	832	7370	9002	832
8414	**587**	612	NC	428	7320	9018	428
8026	**745**	727	EW70	741	7503	8058	741
8108	**867**	472	NC	205	7165	9620	205
8794	277	300	**EW30**	456	7708	8528	456
navy	A5	320	NC	**106**	7023	8638	106

75. Chicory

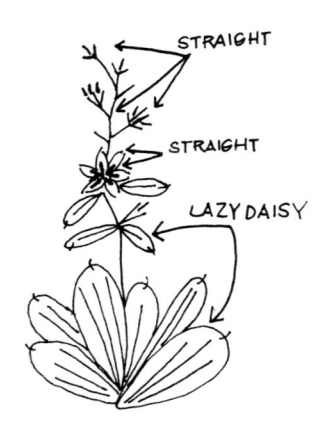

Stem and Leaves
Gumnut: green 547

Flowers and Buds
Gumnut: dark blue 389; blue 386

1. Work the stem and bud 'greenery' in straight stitches.
2. Form the petals with two, blue straight stitches worked closely together. Work the centre in dark blue straight stitches.
3. Work the buds in blue straight stitch.
4. Work the leaves in lazy daisies filled in with straight stitches.

76. Quaking Grass

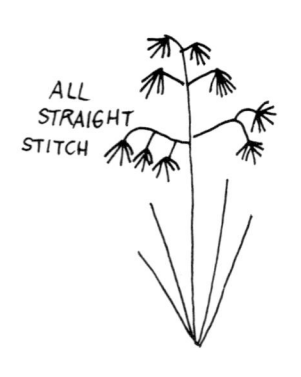

Stems and Leaves
DMC Medici: dark brown 8839; green 8413

Spikelets
DMC Medici: tan 8308

1. Work the stems and spikelet casings in dark brown straight stitches.
2. Work the leaves in green straight stitch.
3. Form the spikelets with tan straight stitches worked at right angles to each other.

77. Barley

Stems and Leaves
DMC Medici: old gold 8327

Spikelets
DMC Medici: yellow 8027; old gold 8327
DMC stranded cotton: gold 676

1. Work the stems and leaves in straight stitches.
2. Work the spikelets in old gold lazy daisies filled in with one or two, yellow straight stitches. Complete the spikelets by working a straight stitch over the end of each spike with a single strand of gold cotton.

78. Clover

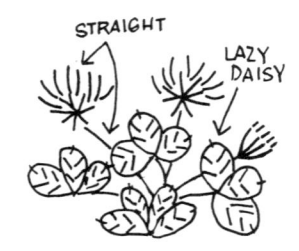

Stems and Leaves
Gumnut green: 587

Flowers and Bud
Gumnut: blush pink 010
DMC Medici: tan 8308

1. Work the stems, bud and bud 'greenery' in straight stitches.
2. Work the flowers in straight stitches, working the blush pink first then adding the tan over the top.
3. Form the leaves with lazy daisies filled in with straight stitches worked at right angles.

79. Rush

Stems and Leaves
DMC Medici: green 8344

Flowers
DMC Medici: brown 8610

1. Work each stem with two straight stitches.
2. Work the flowers in straight stitch.
3. Work the leaves in split stitch.

80. Wild Oat

Stem
DMC Medici: soft green 8420

Spikelets
DMC Medici: dark gold 8304
DMC stranded cotton: brown 434

1. Work the stems and 'green' of the spikelets in straight stitches.
2. Work the spikelets in dark gold straight stitches. Complete the spikelets with straight stitches using a single strand of brown stranded cotton.

DMC Medici	Gumnut	Paterna	RoyalStitch	Appletons Crewel	DMC Tapestry	Anchor Tapestry	Appletons Tapestry
8027	708	713	NC	552	7727	8114	552
8304	C5	D531	NC	312	7485	8020	312
8308	645	643	NC	952	7413	9326	952
8327	745	743	NC	472	7078	8040	472
8344	608	691	NC	545	7045	9100	545
8413	606	D522	NC	831	7542	9004	831
8420	675	635	NC	251A	7340	9194	251A
8610	927	452	EW87	914	7513	8048	914
8839	967	471	NC	185	7060	9640	185
8118	**010**	948	EW23	881	7300	8292	881
8798	**386**	544	EW43	462	7798	8688	462
8720	**389**	541	EW40	464	7797	8690	464
8415	**547**	661	NC	832	7541	8992	832
8414	**587**	612	NC	428	7320	9018	428

81. Fescue

Stems and Leaves
DMC Medici: light green 8369; green 8413; tan 8308

Spikelets
DMC Medici: green 8413

1. Work the stems in green straight stitch.
2. Form the spikelets with clusters of two straight stitches worked closely together.
3. Work the leaves in light green and tan straight stitch.

82. Wheat

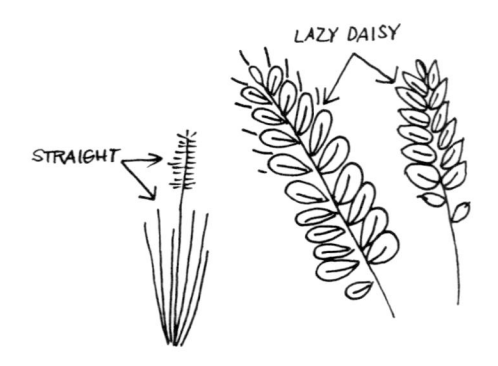

Stems and Leaves
DMC Medici: gold 8303A

Spikelets
DMC Medici: gold 8303A; light gold 8326

1. Work the stems and leaves in straight stitches.
2. Form the spikelets with gold lazy daisies filled in with light gold straight stitches.
3. Work some extra straight stitches at the top.

83. False Foxtail

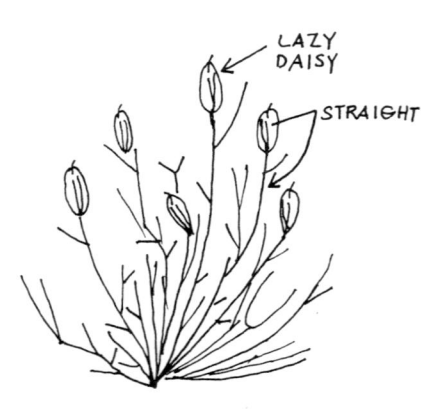

Stems and Leaves
DMC Medici: soft blue green 8426

Spikelets
DMC Medici: dark blue green 8203

1. Work the stems and leaves in straight stitch.
2. Work the spikelets in lazy daisies filled in with straight stitches.

84. Sharp Rush

Stems
Gumnut: green 567

Flowers
DMC Medici: brown 8321

1. Work the stems in straight stitch.
2. Work the flowers in clusters of pistil stitch.

85. Meadow Grass

The Plant
DMC Medici: green 8419

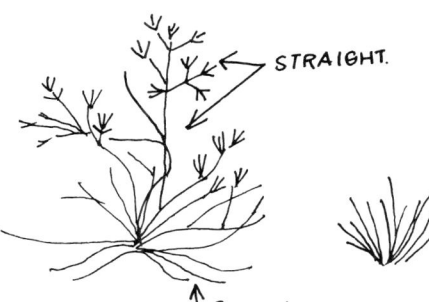

1. Work the base of the plant in stem stitch.
2. Work very small clusters of straight stitch at the ends of some of the 'stems'.

DMC Medici	Gumnut	Paterna	RoyalStitch	Appletons Crewel	DMC Tapestry	Anchor Tapestry	Appletons Tapestry
8203	05	D546	NC	155	7337	8880	155
8303A	C4	702	NC	726	7473	9524	726
8308	645	643	NC	952	7413	9326	952
8321	927	441	NC	902	7477	8044	902
8326	745	703	NC	692	7503	8040	692
8369	604	605	NC	401	7402	9014	401
8413	606	D522	NC	831	7542	9004	831
8419	616	693	NC	253	7548	9164	253
8426	AP2	D556	NC	152	7321	8874	152
8406	567	662	NC	833	7386	9004	833

86. Great Millet

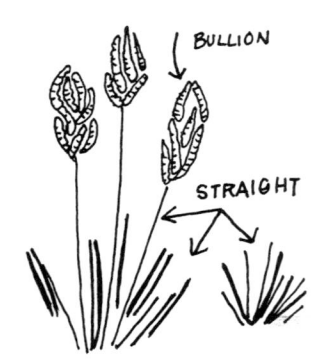

Stems and Leaves
Gumnut: green 567;
pale green 542

Seedheads
DMC Medici: soft mauve 8120A

1. Work the stems in green straight stitch.
2. Work the leaves in either green or pale green straight stitch.
3. Work the seedheads in eight- or ten-wrap bullions.

87. Cocksfoot

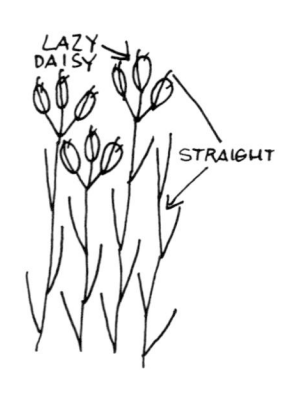

The Plant
DMC Medici: green 8406

1. Work the stems and leaves in straight stitches.
2. Form the spikelets with a lazy daisy with a straight stitch centre. Complete the spikelet by working a straight stitch over the point of the lazy daisy. (See Stitch Glossary.)

DMC Medici	Gumnut	Paterna	RoyalStitch	Appletons Crewel	DMC Tapestry	Anchor Tapestry	Appletons Tapestry
8120A	966	D133	NC	220	7949	9618	220
8406	586	602	NC	832	7370	9078	832
8871	542	665	NC	522	7040	8982	522
8406	567	662	NC	833	7386	9004	833

Australian Natives

North American Wildflowers

Australian Natives
88. Flannel Flower
89. Kangaroo paw
90. Christmas Bells
91. Spider Orchid
92. Tea Tree
93. Wattle
94. Red Flowering Gum
95. Boronia
96. Banksia
97. Rabbit Orchid
98. Tasmanian Waratah
99. Yellow Grevillea
100. Bottlebrush
101. Everlasting Daisy
102. Sturts Desert Pea

88. Flannel Flower	89. Kangaroo paw	90. Christmas Bells	91. Spider Orchid	92. Tea Tree
93. Wattle	94. Red Flowering Gum	95. Boronia	96. Banksia	97. Rabbit Orchid
98. Tasmanian Waratah	99. Yellow Grevillea	100. Bottlebrush	101. Everlasting Daisy	102. Sturts Desert Pea

North American Wildflowers
103. Spiderwort
104. Trillium
105. Carolina Jasmine
106. Mountain Pasque Flower
107. Deptford pink
108. Black-eyed Susan
109. Shooting Star
110. Texas Bluebonnet
111. Spotted Knapweed
112. Goldenrod
113. Cardinal Flower
114. lilac
115. Sunflower
116. Indian paintbrush
117. Indian blanket

103. Spiderwort	104. Trillium	105. Carolina Jasmine	106. Mountain Pasque Flower	107. Deptford pink
108. Black-eyed Susan	109. Shooting Star	110. Texas Bluebonnet	111. Spotted Knapweed	112. Goldenrod
113. Cardinal Flower	114. lilac	115. Sunflower	116. Indian paintbrush	117. Indian blanket

Australian Natives

88
89
90
91
92
93
94
95
96
97
98
99
100
101
102

North American Wildflowers

56

88. Flannel Flower

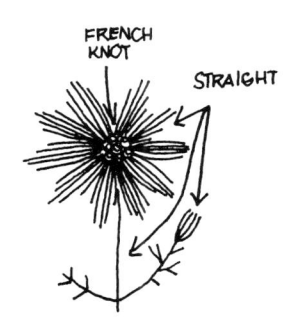

Stem and Leaves
Gumnut: green 566

Flower and Bud
DMC Medici: cream 8328; sand 8421

1. Work the stem in a straight stitch.
2. Form the ten petals with five, cream straight stitches worked closely together. Work the central stitch first and then place two stitches either side.
3. Form the centre of the flower with sand, single-twist French knots.
4. Work the sand bud and leaves in straight stitches.

89. Kangaroo Paw

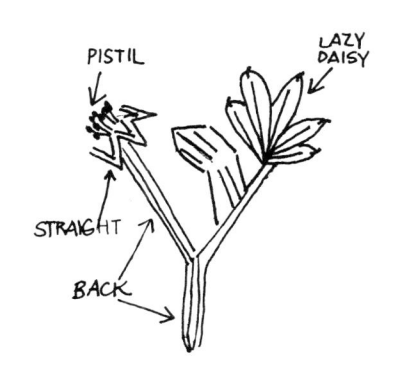

Stem
Gumnut: light green C3

Flower and Buds
Gumnut: sandstone C4
DMC Medici: bright green 8341

1. Work the stem in long back stitches.
2. Work the open flower in bright green straight stitch and pistil stitch.
3. Work the buds in sandstone lazy daisies with straight stitch centres.

90. Christmas Bells

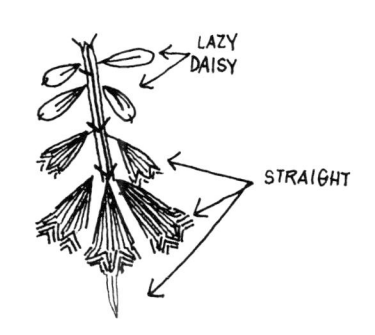

Stem and Buds
DMC Medici: garnet 8102

Flowers
DMC Medici: red 8127; yellow 8026

1. Form the stem with three straight stitches worked closely together.
2. Work the buds in garnet lazy daisies filled in with straight stitches.
3. Outline the flower in red straight stitches and fill in. Work small, yellow straight stitches at the opening of each flower.
4. Complete by working a small, garnet straight stitch at the base of each flower and bud.

DMC Medici	Gumnut	Paterna	RoyalStitch	Appletons Crewel	DMC Tapestry	Anchor Tapestry	Appletons Tapestry
8026	708	712	EW70	553	7726	8118	553
8102	038	950	NC	505	7108	8220	505
8127	857	970	NC	504	7666	8222	504
8328	743	715	NC	841	7579	8012	841
8341	678	692	NC	253	7341	9152	253
8421	642	644	NC	331	7371	9172	331
8400	**C3**	653	NC	693	7422	9304	693
8400	**C4**	652	NC	694	7362	8040	694
8406	**566**	664	NC	832	7370	9002	832

91. Spider Orchid

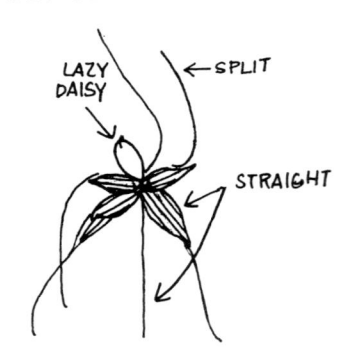

Stem and Flower
DMC Medici: brown 8108; pale pink 8505A

1. Work the stem in a straight stitch.
2. Work the top petal in a pale pink lazy daisy.
3. Work the broader section of the other petals in pale pink straight stitches. Work the finer ends of the petals in brown split stitch.

92. Tea Tree

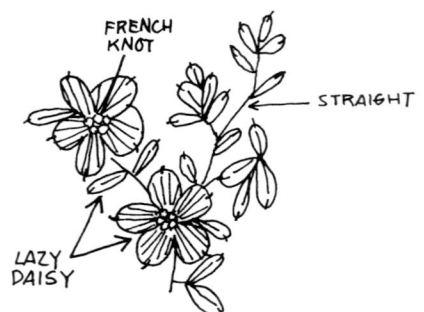

Stems and Leaves
Gumnut: mushroom 966
DMC Medici: green 8413

Flowers and Bud
Gumnut: pale pink 191; deep pink 157

1. Work the stems in mushroom straight stitch.
2. Form the flower by working deep pink, single-twist French knots in the centre. Work the petals and bud in pale pink lazy daisies filled in with three straight stitches.
3. Work the leaves in a green lazy daisy with a straight stitch centre.

93. Wattle

Stem and Leaves
Gumnut: mushroom 966; green 635

Flowers
Anchor tapestry: yellow 8114

1. Work the stem in a mushroom straight stitch.
2. Work the leaves in green split stitch.
3. Form each cluster by working three turkey knots very, very close together. Cut and fluff the turkey knots.

94. Red Flowering Gum

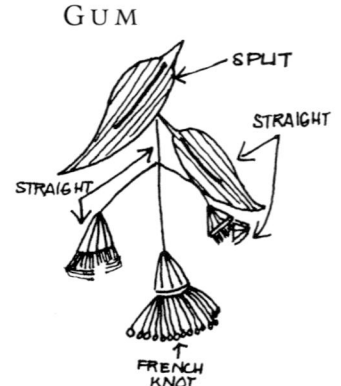

Leaves
DMC Medici: green 8414
DMC Medici: red 8666

Flowers and bud
Gumnut: beige 643
DMC Medici: red 8666; yellow 8026

1. Work the stem and the top of the flowers and bud in beige straight stitches.
2. Work the flowers and buds in red straight stitches. Complete the open flower by working yellow, single-twist French knots.
3. Outline the leaves in split stitch and fill in with straight stitches. Complete the leaves by working a red straight stitch to form the central vein.

95. BORONIA

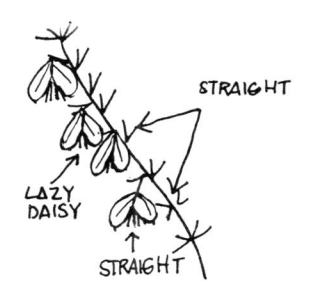

Stem and Leaves
DMC Medici: dark brown 8839; green 8344

Flowers
DMC Medici: burgundy 8106; yellow 8026

1. Work the stem in a dark brown straight stitch.
2. Work the flowers by first working the yellow 'underneath' with yellow straight stitches. Work the 'over' petals in burgundy lazy daisies with straight stitch centres.
3. Work the leaves in green straight stitch.

96. BANKSIA

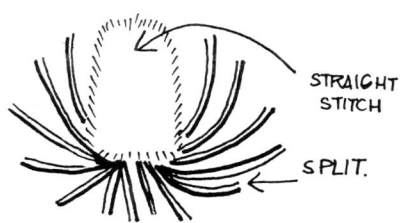

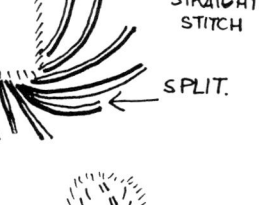

Leaves
Gumnut: green 547

Flower
Gumnut: lemon 745
DMC Medici: yellow 8027 & 8748

1. Work the foundation of the flower in lemon straight stitch. (See diagram A.)
2. Form each leaf by working two rows of split stitch.
3. Complete the flower by working a lot of small straight stitches in the two fine yellow wools. (See diagram B.) Only work with one colour at a time.

DMC Medici	Gumnut	Paterna	RoyalStitch	Appletons Crewel	DMC Tapestry	Anchor Tapestry	Appletons Tapestry
8026	708	712	EW70	553	7726	8118	553
8027	708	713	NC	552	7727	8114	552
8106	H5	D211	NC	505	7147	8402	505
8108	907	403	NC	124	7063	9512	124
8344	608	691	NC	545	7045	9100	545
8413	606	D522	NC	403	7542	9004	403
8414	B5	610	NC	295	7385	9008	295
8505A	943	406	NC	701	7171	9502	701
8666	038	970	NC	501	7666	8202	501
8748	706	714	EW73	551	7078	8014	551
8839	967	471	NC	185	7060	9640	185
8212	**157**	900	NC	146	7139	8424	146
8225	**191**	964	NC	751	7200	8542	751
8415	**547**	661	NC	832	7541	8992	832
8406	**635**	604	NC	352	7704	9066	352
8421	**643**	644	EW63	331A	7371	9302	331A
8026	**745**	727	NC	741	7503	8508	741
8840	**966**	D143	NC	121	7230	9656	121
8027	708	772	NC	552	7431	**8114**	552

97. Rabbit Orchid

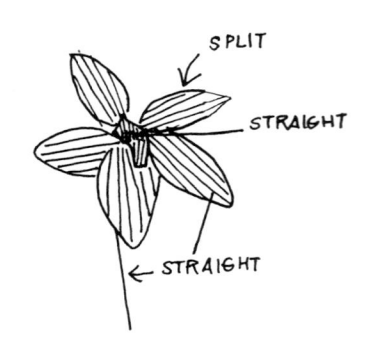

Stem
Gumnut: green 566

Flower
DMC Medici: bright pink 8153; dark pink 8685; white

1. Work the stem in a straight stitch.
2. Work the outline of the petals in bright pink split stitch and fill in with straight stitches.
3. Work the centre in white straight stitches and work dark pink straight stitches either side.

98. Tasmanian Waratah

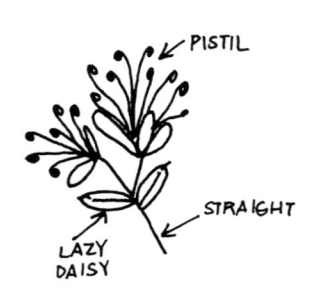

Stems and Leaves
DMC Medici: green 8414

Flower
Appletons crewel wool: red 448

1. Work the stems in straight stitch.
2. Work the flowers in pistil stitch.
3. Work the leaves in a lazy daisy with a straight stitch centre.

99. Yellow Grevillea

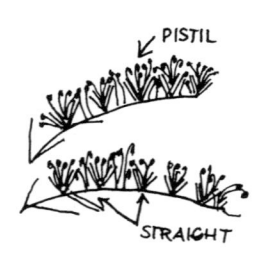

Stems and Leaves
DMC Medici: dark brown 8839; green 8344

Flowers
DMC Medici: yellow 8026

1. Work the stems in dark brown split stitch.
2. Work the base of each flower in dark brown straight stitch.
3. Work the flowers in clusters of pistil stitch.
4. Work the leaves in green straight stitch.

100. Bottlebrush

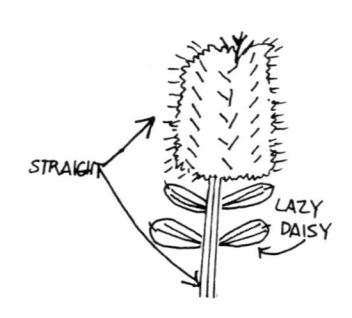

Stem and Leaves
DMC Medici: green 8344

Flower
DMC Medici: red 8666; green 8344

1. Work the stem in three straight stitches.
2. Work the flower in horizontal and diagonal straight stitches. Complete the flower by working green straight stitches at the top.
3. Work the leaves in lazy daisies filled in with straight stitches.

101. EVERLASTING DAISY

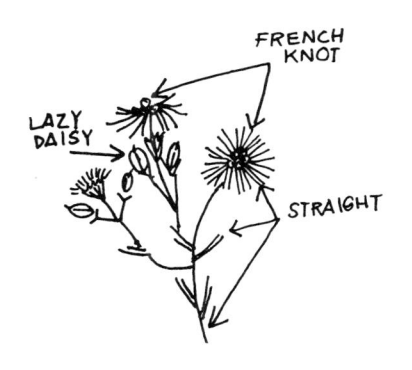

Stems and Leaves
DMC Medici: green 8419;

Flowers and Buds
Gumnut: yellow 708
DMC Medici: orange 8941; sand 8421
dark yellow 8725

1. Work the stems and bud 'greenery' in straight stitches.
2. Form the centre of the flower with orange, single-twist French knots.
3. Work the petals in yellow straight stitches.
4. Work the bases of the flowers in sand straight stitches.
5. Work the buds in a dark yellow lazy daisy with a straight stitch centre.
6. Form the leaves with two, green straight stitches worked closely together.

102. STURT'S DESERT PEA

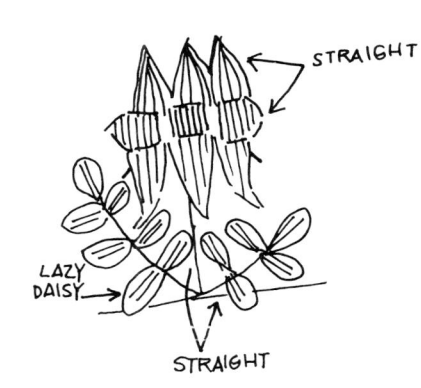

Stems and Leaves
Gumnut: green 566

Flowers
Appletons crewel wool: red 447;
black 998; navy 106

1. Work the stems in straight stitch.
2. Work the flower in straight stitch. First work the red then work the centres with a strand of black and navy in the needle together.
3. Form the leaves with a lazy daisy filled in with straight stitches.

DMC Medici	Gumnut	Paterna	RoyalStitch	Appletons Crewel	DMC Tapestry	Anchor Tapestry	Appletons Tapestry
white	990	261	NC	991B	white	8004	991B
8026	360	712	EW70	553	7726	8118	553
8153	196	353	NC	801	7153	8488	801
8344	608	691	NC	545	7045	9100	545
8414	B5	661	NC	833	7540	9022	833
8419	616	693	NC	253	7548	9164	253
8421	643	644	NC	331	7371	9172	331
8666	038	970	NC	501	7666	8202	501
8685	077	903	NC	803	7600	8458	803
8725	708	613	NC	554	7742	8120	554
8839	967	471	NC	185	7060	9640	185
8941	827	812	NC	557	7051	8156	557
8325	**708**	771	NC	555	7056	8122	555
8406	**566**	664	NC	832	7370	9002	832
navy	A5	320	NC	**106**	7023	8638	106
8103	827	840	NC	**447**	7666	8198	447
8127	827	970	NC	**448**	7849	8200	448
8713	998	221	NC	**998**	7624	9800	998

AUSTRALIAN NATIVES

103. Spiderwort

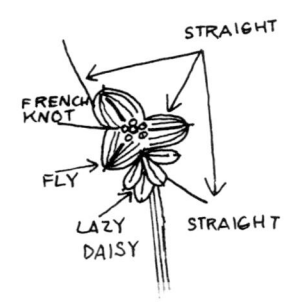

Stem and Leaves
DMC Medici: dark green 8403

Flower
RoyalStitch: purple EW30
Appletons crewel wool: navy 465
DMC Medici: dark yellow 8725

1. Work the stem in three straight stitches.
2. Form the outer edge of each petal with a purple fly stitch and fill in with straight stitches.
3. Work the centre of each petal in a navy straight stitch.
4. Form the central stamen with a navy, double-twist French knot and surround it with dark yellow single-twist French knots.
5. Complete the flower with green lazy daisies with straight stitch centres, and two long straight stitches.

104. Trillium

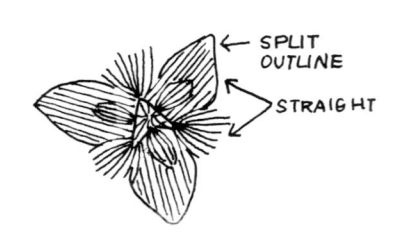

Leaves
DMC Medici: green 8419; dark green 8403

Flower
DMC Medici: raspberry 8101; old gold 8327; white;

1. Outline the larger leaves in dark green split stitch and fill in with straight stitches.
2. Work the smaller leaves in green straight stitches.
3. Work the three, white petals in straight stitches.
4. Work the centre of the flower in a triangle of raspberry straight stitches. Fill in with old gold straight stitches.

105. Carolina Jasmine

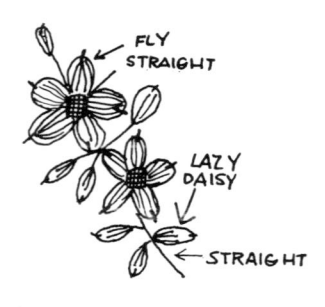

Stem and Leaves
DMC Medici: green 8344

Flowers and Bud
DMC Medici: yellow 8026

1. Work the stem in a straight stitch.
2. Using two strands of yellow form the centre by working four, horizontal straight stitches close together and then four vertical stitches over the top.
3. Form the petals with a fly stitch filled in with three straight stitches.
4. Work the leaves and buds in lazy daisies filled in with straight stitches.

106. Mountain Pasque Flower

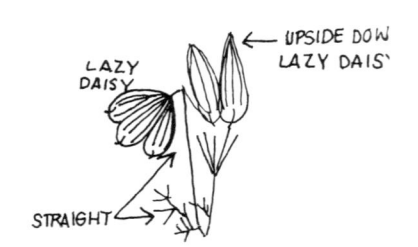

Stem and Leaves
DMC Medici: green 8346

Flowers
Gumnut: purple 257

1. Work the stem and leaves in straight stitches.
2. Form the flower by working three lazy daisies filled in with straight stitches.
3. Work the partly open flower in two lazy daisies which are started at the top.

62 NORTH AMERICAN WILDFLOWERS

107. DEPTFORD PINK

Stem and Leaves
DMC Medici: dark green 8409

Flower and Bud
DMC Medici: dark green 8409
dark pink 8685

1. Work the stem in a straight stitch.
2. Work the petals in dark pink, 'plump' lazy daisies filled in with straight stitches. Complete the flower by working six, dark green, single-twist French knots in the centre.
3. Work the leaves, base of the flower and bud in straight stitches.

108. BLACK-EYED SUSAN

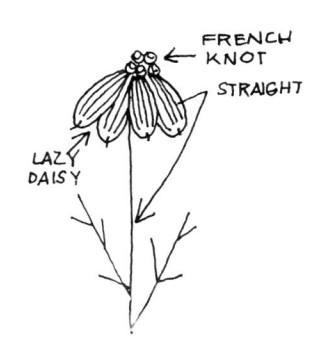

Stem and Leaves
Gumnut: green 586

Flower
Gumnut: yellow 708; brown 987

1. Work the stem and leaves in straight stitches.
2. Form the petals with yellow lazy daisies filled in with straight stitches.
3. Form the stamens with brown, single-twist French knots

DMC Medici	Gumnut	Paterna	RoyalStitch	Appletons Crewel	DMC Tapestry	Anchor Tapestry	Appletons Tapestry
white	990	261	NC	991B	white	8004	991B
8026	708	712	EW70	553	7726	8118	553
8101	097	901	NC	758	7138	8458	758
8327	745	743	NC	472	7078	8040	472
8344	608	691	NC	545	7045	9100	545
8346	616	692	NC	544	7769	9102	544
8403	608	691	NC	256	7320	9206	256
8409	B5	531	NC	158	7329	8884	158
8419	616	693	NC	253	7548	9164	253
8685	077	903	NC	803	7600	8458	803
8725	708	613	NC	554	7742	8120	554
8895	**257**	332	NC	895	7711	8590	895
8125	**987**	D115	NC	584	7416	8512	584
8413	**586**	613	NC	425	7384	9016	425
8026	**708**	726	EW70	553	7055	8118	553
8794	277	300	**EW30**	456	7708	8528	456
8720	A5	571	NC	**465**	7823	8694	465

NORTH AMERICAN WILDFLOWERS

109. SHOOTING STAR

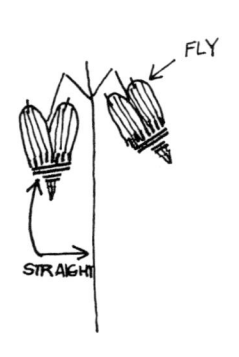

Stems
DMC Medici: brown 8108

Flowers
DMC Medici: hot pink 8155; white; dark yellow 8725; dark brown 8306

1. Work the stems in straight stitch.
2. Form the shape of the two petals with hot pink fly stitch filled in with straight stitches.
3. To complete the flower work a row of white, vertical straight stitches, three, dark yellow horizontal straight stitches, and three dark brown vertical straight stitches.

110. TEXAS BLUEBONNET

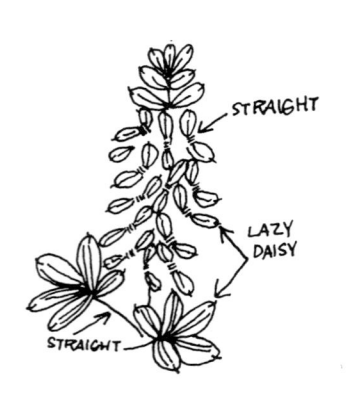

Stem and Leaves
DMC Medici: green 8344

Flower
DMC Medici: navy 8720; light blue 8799; cream 8328

1. Work the stem in a straight stitch.
2. Work the buds at the top of the flower in lazy daisies with straight stitch centres using the cream first, then light blue and navy.
3. Form the flowerets with navy lazy daisies filled in with straight stitches. Work three cream straight stitches over the centre of each floweret.
4. Form the leaves with lazy daisies filled in with straight stitches.

111. SPOTTED KNAPWEED

Stems and Leaves
DMC Medici: green 8406

Flowers
DMC Medici: light pink 8151; bright pink 8153

1. Work the stems leaves and base of the flowers in straight stitches.
2. Form the flower by working light pink straight stitches from the base. Complete the flower with longer bright pink straight stitches worked over the light pink.

112. GOLDENROD

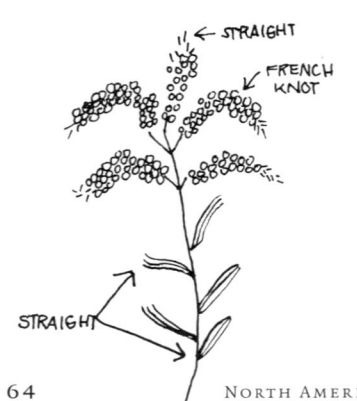

Stem and Leaves
Gumnut: green 616

Flowers
RoyalStitch: dark yellow EW70

1. Work the stem in a straight stitch.
2. Work the flowers with double-twist French knots.
3. Work some very small straight stitches at the end of each cluster.
4. Form the leaves with three straight stitches worked very closely together.

64   North American Wildflowers

113. CARDINAL FLOWER

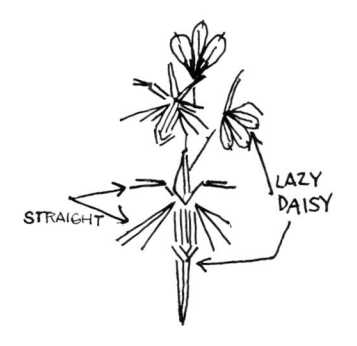

Stem
DMC Medici: green 8418

Flowers and Buds
DMC Medici: red 8666; burgundy 8106

1. Form the stem with three straight stitches worked very closely together.
2. Form the central petal of the full-view flowers with a red, 'plump' lazy daisy filled in with straight stitches. Form the remaining petals with straight stitches.
3. Work the side-view flower in three lazy daisies. Fill in and complete the flower with straight stitches.
4. Work the buds in burgundy lazy daisies filled in with straight stitches.

114. LILAC

Stems and Leaves
DMC Medici: green 8346

Flower
Gumnut: light lilac 255; dark lilac 235

1. Work the stems in straight stitch.
2. Form the open flowerets with light lilac straight stitches using two strands of wool.
3. Work the buds in dark lilac, single-twist French knots.
4. Form the leaves with lazy daisies.

DMC Medici	Gumnut	Paterna	RoyalStitch	Appletons Crewel	DMC Tapestry	Anchor Tapestry	Appletons Tapestry
white	990	261	NC	991B	white	8004	991B
8106	857	D211	NC	505	7147	8402	505
8108	907	403	NC	124	7063	9512	124
8151	054	904	NC	943	7151	8454	943
8153	196	353	NC	801	7153	8488	801
8155	057	903	NC	755	7602	8456	755
8306	AP5	410	NC	187	7479	9644	187
8328	743	715	NC	841	7579	8012	841
8344	608	691	NC	545	7045	9100	545
8346	616	692	NC	544	7769	9102	544
8406	586	602	NC	832	7370	9078	832
8418	607	692	NC	254	7547	9168	254
8666	827	970	NC	501	7666	8202	501
8720	389	541	EW40	824	7797	8690	824
8725	708	613	EW70	554	7742	8120	554
8799	364	545	NC	462	7799	8684	462
8332	**255**	334	NC	884	7241	8586	884
8419	**616**	693	NC	544	7769	9100	554
8896	**235**	313	NC	603	7014	8544	603
8026	745	727	**EW70**	741	7055	8058	741

115. SUNFLOWER

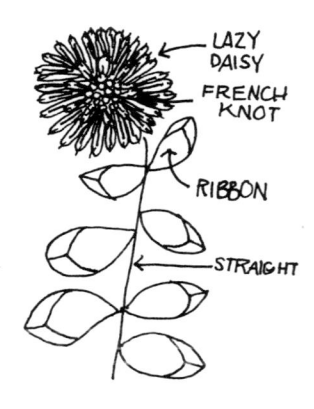

Stem and Leaves
Gumnut: green 586
YLI silk ribbon: 7 mm green 20

Flower
DMC Medici: dark yellow 8725; yellow 8027
Gumnut: brown 987

1. Work the stem in a straight stitch.
2. Work one round of dark yellow lazy daisies with straight stitch centres. Work the lazy daisies closely together.
3. Work an inner round of yellow lazy daisies.
4. Complete the flower by working brown, single-twist French knots in the centre.
5. Work the leaves in ribbon stitch with silk ribbon.

116. INDIAN PAINTBRUSH

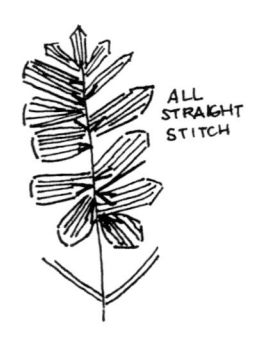

Stem and Leaves
DMC Medici: dark green 8403

Flower and Buds
Gumnut: red 039; brown 987

1. Work the stem in a straight stitch.
2. Work the larger flowerets by outlining their shape in red straight stitch and filling in with straight stitches.
3. Work the buds, brown accents to the flowerets, and leaves in two straight stitches worked closely together.

117. INDIAN BLANKET

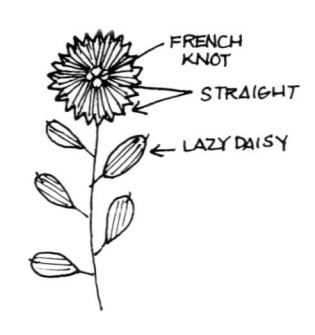

Stem and Leaves
DMC Medici: green 8418

Flower
DMC Medici: rust 8126; dark yellow 8725; burgundy 8106

1. Work the stem in a straight stitch.
2. Work the inner section of the petals in rust straight stitches using two strands of wool.
3. Work the tips in dark yellow straight stitch.
4. Work the centre of the flower in burgundy, single-twist French knots using two strands of wool.
5. Form the leaves with lazy daisies filled in with straight stitches.

DMC Medici	Gumnut	Paterna	RoyalStitch	Appletons Crewel	DMC Tapestry	Anchor Tapestry	Appletons Tapestry
8027	708	713	NC	552	7727	8114	552
8106	857	D211	NC	505	7147	8402	505
8126	H5	840	NC	503	7107	8204	503
8403	608	691	NC	256	7320	9206	256
8418	607	692	NC	254	7547	9168	254
8725	708	613	EW70	554	7742	8120	554
8127	**039**	971	NC	502	7544	8202	502
8125	**987**	D115	NC	584	7416	8512	584
8413	**586**	613	NC	425	7384	9016	425

66 NORTH AMERICAN WILDFLOWERS

BLOSSOM GARLAND, ROSES

FUCHSIA AND WISTERIA GARLAND

BLOSSOM GARLAND
118. Blanket Stitch
119. Double Lazy Daisy
120. Coral Stitch
121. Whipped Stitch

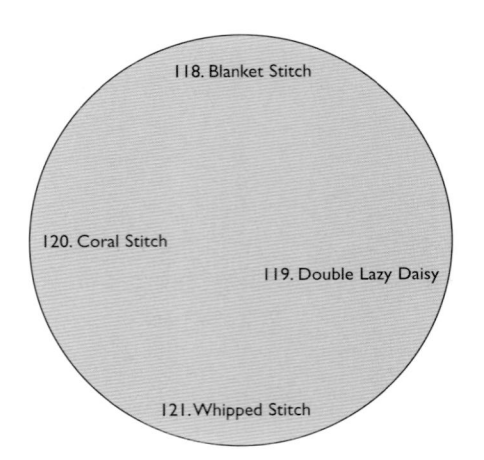

118. Blanket Stitch
120. Coral Stitch
119. Double Lazy Daisy
121. Whipped Stitch

ROSES 1
122 – 125. Stem Stitch
126 – 129. Chain Stitch
130 – 133. Lazy Daisy
134 – 137. Coral Stitch
138 – 141. Woven Roses
142 – 145. Back Stitch

122 – 125. Stem Stitch
126 – 129. Chain Stitch
130 – 133. Lazy Daisy
134 – 137. Coral Stitch
138 – 141. Woven Roses
142 – 145. Back Stitch

ROSES 2
146 – 149. Coral and Stem Stitch
150 – 153. Double Lazy daisy
154 – 157. Ribbed Wheel
158 – 161. Bullion
162 – 165. Blanket Stitch
166 – 169. Bullion

146 – 149. Coral and Stem Stitch
150 – 153. Double Lazy daisy
154 – 157. Ribbed Wheel
158 – 161. Bullion
162 – 165. Blanket Stitch
166 – 169. Bullion

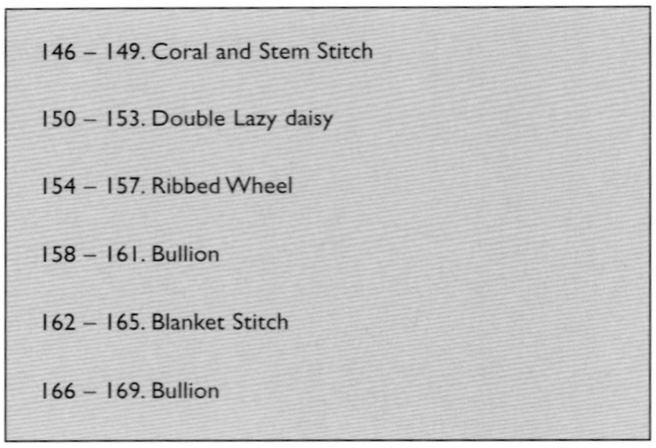

FUCHSIA AND WISTERIA GARLAND
170. Beauty of Bath
171. La Rosita
172. Hazel
173. Lollipop
174. Native Dancer
175. Blue Sleigh Bells
176 – 178. Wisteria

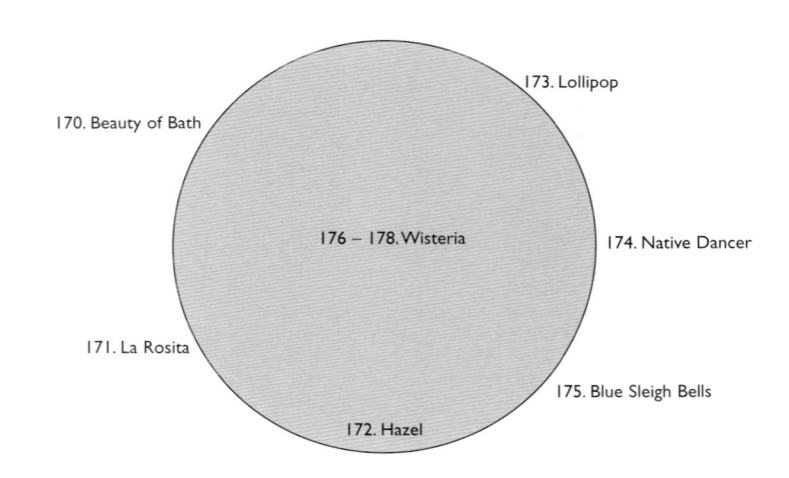

173. Lollipop
170. Beauty of Bath
176 – 178. Wisteria
174. Native Dancer
171. La Rosita
175. Blue Sleigh Bells
172. Hazel

Blossom Garland

Roses 1

122
123
124
125
126
127
128
129
130
131
132
133
134
135
136
137
138
139
140
141
142
143
144
145

Roses 2

146 147 148 149
150 151 152 153
154 155 156 157
158 159 160 161
162 163 164 165
166 167 168 169

Fuchsia and Wisteria garland

BLOSSOM GARLAND

Stems and Leaves
Anchor tapestry: green 9016; brown 9646
YLI silk ribbon 7 mm: green 32

118. 'Blanket Stitch' Blossom

Flowers and Buds
Anchor tapestry: rose pink 8396
light pink 8392

1. Work the stems in brown and green straight stitches.
2. To form the flower work a circle of light pink blanket stitch. Weave over and under the bars of the blanket stitch to fill in the flower. (I have woven a row of rose pink near the outer edge of one of the flowers.)
3. Work the rose pink, side-view flower in four lazy daisies with straight stitch centres.
4. Work the light pink, side-view flower in blanket stitch and weave as explained in 2 above.
5. Work the buds in two to four straight stitches.
6. Work the bud 'greenery' in green straight stitches.
7. Work the leaves in ribbon stitch with silk ribbon.

119. 'Double Lazy Daisy' Blossom

Flowers and Buds
Anchor tapestry: peach 8302

1. Work the stems and bud 'greenery' in green straight stitches.
2. Work the side-view and full-view flowers in double lazy daisies with straight stitch centres.
3. Form the buds with either a lazy daisy or a double-twist French knot.
4. Work the leaves in ribbon stitch with silk ribbon.

120. 'Coral Stitch' Blossom

Flowers and Buds
Anchor tapestry: pink 8434

1. Work the stems and bud 'greenery' in green straight stitches.
2. Work two to three rounds of coral stitch. Complete the flower by 'over stitching' in straight stitches.
3. Form the buds with a straight stitch over the point of a lazy daisy. (See Stitch Glossary.)
4. Work the leaves in ribbon stitch with silk ribbon.

121. 'Whipped Stitch' Blossom

Flowers and Buds
Anchor tapestry: deep pink 8440;
    light pink 8392
YLI sparkling organdy 9 mm: pink 3

1. Work the stems and bud 'greenery' in brown and green straight stitches.
2. Form the flowers with five or six rounds of light pink running stitch. Whip the rounds with sparkling organdy. Complete the flower with either a light or deep pink French knot.
3. Work the buds in lazy daisies with a straight stitch centre.
4. Work the leaves in ribbon stitch with silk ribbon.

BLOSSOM GARLAND

DMC Medici	Gumnut	Paterna	RoyalStitch	Appletons Crewel	DMC Tapestry	Anchor Tapestry	Appletons Tapestry
8139	804	874	NC	708	7122	**8302**	708
8818	150	964	EW23	751	7003	**8392**	751
8816	855	945	EW20	943	7760	**8396**	943
8816	035	963	NC	944	7105	**8434**	944
8817	058	942	NC	947	7640	**8440**	947
8406	566	603	NC	401	7369	**9016**	401
8306	967	422	NC	581	7801	**9646**	581

Roses

I have included the following 48 roses to show you the effects when using either one or two strands of crewel wool or one strand of tapestry wool. I have indicated the colours I used but have not included conversion charts. This allows you to make your own colour selection.

As you can see tapestry wools give a larger and more textured rose. The various stitches I have used give a different shape to the roses, for example, the 'chain stitch' roses (nos 122–125) are similar to an old fashioned damask rose while the 'bullion' roses (nos 158–161) are similar to the 'Peace' rose.

'Stem Stitch' Roses

Gumnut: pink 054; yellow 726
Anchor tapestry: pink 8484

122.
1. Using two strands of crewel wool form the centre with three, yellow, double-twist French knots.
2. Using one strand of crewel wool complete the rose with two rounds of stem stitch.

123.
This rose has been worked with two strands of crewel wool.
1. Form the centre with three, yellow, double-twist French knots.
2. Complete the rose with two rounds of stem stitch.

124.
1. Using two strands of crewel wool form the centre with three, yellow, double-twist French knots.
2. Using one strand of tapestry wool complete the rose with one round of stem stitch.

125.
1. Using two strands of crewel wool form the centre with four, yellow, double-twist French knots.
2. Using one strand of tapestry wool complete the rose with two rounds of stem stitch.

'Chain Stitch' Roses

Gumnut: dark pink 057; yellow 726
Anchor tapestry: deep pink 8440

126.
1. Using two strands of crewel wool form the centre with three, yellow, double-twist French knots.
2. Using one strand of crewel wool complete the rose with two rounds of chain stitch.

127.
This rose has been worked with two strands of crewel wool.
1. Form the centre with four, yellow, double-twist French knots.
2. Complete the rose with three rounds of chain stitch.

128. 
1. Using two strands of crewel wool form the centre with four, yellow, double-twist French knots.
2. Using one strand of tapestry wool complete the rose with two rounds of chain stitch.

129. 
1. Using two strands of crewel wool form the centre with four, yellow, double-twist French knots.
2. Using one strand of tapestry wool complete the rose with three rounds of chain stitch.

'LAZY DAISY' ROSES

Gumnut: gold 728
Anchor tapestry: gold 8060; green 9016

130.  Using one strand of crewel wool work the rose in five lazy daisies filled in with two straight stitches.

131.  Using two strands of crewel wool work the rose in five lazy daisies filled in with two straight stitches.

132.  Using one strand of tapestry wool work the rose in five lazy daisies filled in with two straight stitches.

133.  Using one strand of tapestry wool work the bud in a lazy daisy with a straight stitch centre. Work the bud 'greenery' in straight stitches.

'CORAL STITCH' ROSES

Gumnut: yellow 726; gold 728
Anchor tapestry: lemon 8056; gold 8060

134.  This rose has been worked with one strand of crewel wool.
1. Form the centre with four, gold, double-twist French knots.
2. Complete the rose with three rounds of yellow, coral stitch.

135. 
1. Using one strand of crewel wool form the centre with four, gold, double-twist French knots.
2. Using two strands of crewel wool complete the rose with three rounds of yellow coral stitch.

ROSES 77

136.  This rose has been worked with one strand of tapestry wool.
1. Form the centre with four, gold, single-twist French knots.
2. Complete the rose with two rounds of lemon coral stitch.

137.  This rose has been worked with one strand of tapestry wool.
1. Form the centre with a lemon, single-twist French knot.
2. Complete the rose with two and a half rounds of lemon coral stitch.

'WOVEN' ROSES

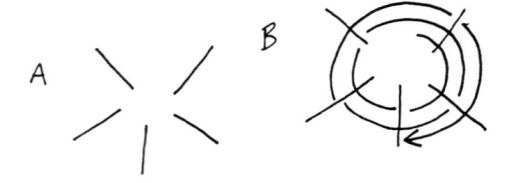

Gumnut: lilac 255; dark purple 299; yellow 726
Anchor tapestry: lilac 8588; purple 8590; dark purple 8594

138. 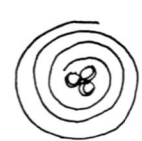 This rose has been worked with one strand of crewel wool.
1. Form the centre with three, yellow, double-twist French knots. Work five straight stitch bars as shown in diagram A.
2. Complete the rose by weaving lilac spiral rounds as shown in diagram B.

139. 
1. Using one strand of crewel wool form the centre with four, dark purple, double-twist French knots. Work five straight stitch bars as shown in diagram A.
2. Using two strands of crewel wool complete the rose by weaving lilac spiral rounds as shown in diagram B.

140. 
1. Using one strand of crewel wool form the centre with four, dark purple, double-twist French knots. Work five straight stitch bars as shown in diagram A.
2. Using one strand of tapestry wool complete the rose by weaving lilac spiral rounds as shown in diagram B.

141.  This rose has been worked with one strand of tapestry wool.
1. Form the centre with three, dark purple, single-twist French knots. Work five straight stitch bars as shown in diagram A.
2. Weave two, purple spiral rounds as shown in diagram B. Complete the rose by weaving lilac spiral rounds.

'BACK STITCH' ROSES

Gumnut: dark purple 299; purple 257
Anchor tapestry: dark purple 8594; purple 8590; green 9106

142.  This rose has been worked with one strand of crewel wool.
1. Form the centre with four, dark purple, double-twist French knots.
2. Complete the rose by working three rounds of dark purple back stitch then three rounds of purple back stitch.

143.  This rose has been worked with two strands of crewel wool.
1. Form the centre with four, dark purple, double-twist French knots.
2. Complete the rose by working four rounds of dark purple back stitch then five rounds of purple back stitch.

144.  This rose has been worked with one strand of tapestry wool.
1. Form the centre with four, dark purple, single-twist French knots.
2. Complete the rose by working two rounds of dark purple back stitch then two rounds of purple back stitch.

145.  Using one strand of tapestry wool form the bud with two, dark purple straight stitches. Work the bud 'greenery' in green straight stitches.

'CORAL & STEM STITCH' ROSES

Gumnut: pink 055
Anchor tapestry: pink 8452

146.  This rose has been worked with one strand of crewel wool.
1. Form the centre with one, double-twist French knot.
2. Complete the rose with two rounds of coral stitch then one round of stem stitch.

147.  This rose has been worked with two strands of crewel wool.
1. Form the centre with three, single-twist French knots.
2. Complete the rose with two rounds of coral stitch then one round of stem stitch.

148.  This rose has been worked with one strand of tapestry wool.
1. Form the centre with three, single-twist French knots.
2. Complete the rose with one round of coral stitch then one round of stem stitch.

149.  This rose has been worked with one strand of tapestry wool.
1. Form the centre with three, double-twist French knots.
2. Complete the rose with two rounds of coral stitch then one round of stem stitch.

'Double Lazy Daisy' Roses

Gumnut: dark pink 057; green 566
Anchor tapestry: pink 8456; green 9100

150. This rose has been worked with one strand of crewel wool.
1. Form the rose with four double lazy daisies with straight stitch centres.
2. Work the 'greenery' in two lazy daisies with a straight stitch centre. Complete the 'greenery' with straight stitches.

151. This rose has been worked with two strands of crewel wool.
1. Form the rose with four double lazy daisies with straight stitch centres.
2. Work the 'greenery' in two lazy daisies with a straight stitch centre. Complete the 'greenery' with straight stitches.

152. This rose has been worked with one strand of tapestry wool.
1. Form the rose with four double lazy daisies with straight stitch centres.
2. Work the 'greenery' in five straight stitches.

153. This rose has been worked with one strand of tapestry wool.
1. Form the bud with a double lazy daisy.
2. Work the bud 'greenery' in four straight stitches.

'Ribbed Wheel' Roses

Gumnut: lemon 706; gold 728
Anchor tapestry: light yellow 8114; gold 8060

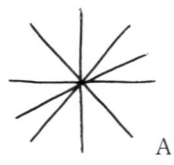

A

154. This rose has been worked with one strand of crewel wool.
1. Work a lemon, ten-spoke base as shown in diagram A.
2. Whip spokes. (See Stitch Glossary.)
3. Place a lemon straight stitch in between each 'roll'.
4. Form the centre with a gold, double-twist French knot.

155. This rose has been worked with two strands of crewel wool.
1. Work a lemon, ten-spoke base as shown in diagram A.
2. Whip spokes. (See Stitch Glossary.)
3. Place a lemon straight stitch in between each 'roll'.
4. Form the centre with three, gold, double-twist French knots.

156.

This rose has been worked with one strand of tapestry wool.
1. Work a light yellow, eight-spoke base as shown in diagram A.
2. Whip spokes. (See Stitch Glossary.)
3. Place a light yellow straight stitch in between each 'roll'.
4. Form the centre with a gold, double-twist French knot.

157.

This rose has been worked with one strand of tapestry wool.
1. Work a light yellow, ten-spoke base as shown in diagram A.
2. Whip spokes. (See Stitch Glossary.)
3. Place a light yellow straight stitch in between each 'roll'.
4. Form the centre with three gold, double-twist French knots.

'BULLION' ROSES (FULL-VIEW)

DMC Medici: yellow 8027; dark yellow 8725
Gumnut: light yellow 706; yellow 708
Anchor tapestry: light yellow; 8114; dark yellow 8118

158.

This rose has been worked with one strand of DMC Medici.
1. Work the centre in three, dark yellow, single-twist French knots.
2. Complete the rose as follows:
   - Round 1: four, six-wrap bullions (dark yellow)
   - Round 2: six, eight-wrap bullions (dark yellow)
   - Round 3: eight, eight-wrap bullions (yellow)
   - Round 4 (half round): three, ten-wrap bullions (yellow).

159.

This rose has been worked with two strands of Gumnut crewel wool.
1. Work the centre in three, yellow, single-twist French knots.
2. Complete the rose as follows:
   - Round 1: four, six-wrap bullions (yellow)
   - Round 2: six, eight-wrap bullions (yellow)
   - Round 3: eight, eight-wrap bullions (light yellow)
   - Round 4 (half round): three, ten-wrap bullions (light yellow).

160.

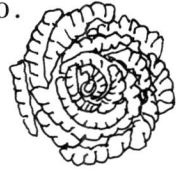

This rose has been worked with one strand of tapestry wool.
1. Work the centre in three, dark yellow, single-twist French knots.
2. Complete the rose as follows:
   - Round 1: three, six-wrap bullions (dark yellow)
   - Round 2: six, seven-wrap bullions (dark yellow)
   - Round 3: eight, seven-wrap bullions (light yellow).

161.

This rose has been worked with one strand of dark yellow tapestry wool.
1. Work the centre in three, single-twist French knots.
2. Complete the rose as follows:
   - Round 1: three, six-wrap bullions
   - Round 2: seven, seven-wrap bullions.

'BLANKET STITCH' ROSES

DMC Medici: blue 8798; dark yellow 8725
Gumnut: blue 386; dark blue 389; gold 728; green 566
Anchor tapestry: light blue 8686; dark blue 8690; gold 8060

162. This rose has been worked with one strand of DMC Medici.
1. Form the outer petals of the rose with a circle of blue, 'wavy' blanket stitch filled in with straight stitches.
2. Work the centre by first working a round of very small, blue blanket stitches and then working three, dark yellow, single-twist French knots.

163. This rose has been worked with one strand of Gumnut crewel wool.
1. Form the outer petals of the rose with a circle of blue, 'wavy' blanket stitch filled in with straight stitches.
2. Work the centre by first working a round of small, dark blue blanket stitches and then working three, gold, single-twist French knots.

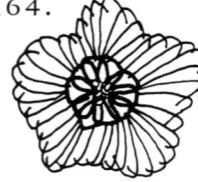

164. This rose has been worked with one strand of tapestry wool.
1. Form the outer petals of the rose with a circle of blue, 'wavy' blanket stitch filled in with straight stitches.
2. Work the centre by first working a round of small, dark blue blanket stitches and then working three, gold, single-twist French knots.

165. These buds have been worked with one strand of Gumnut crewel wool.
1. Form the buds with blue, 'wavy' blanket stitch filled in with straight stitches.
2. Form the bud 'greenery' with straight stitches.

'BULLION STITCH' ROSES (SIDE-VIEW)

DMC Medici: blue 8899
Gumnut: dark blue 389; green 566
Anchor tapestry: blue 8690

166. This rose has been worked with one strand of DMC Medici.
   1. Form the middle of the rose with three, parallel, five-wrap bullions.
   2. Complete the rose by working the following from the middle (in the order given):
      - three, eight-wrap bullions;
      - four, ten-wrap bullions;
      - three, fourteen-wrap bullions.

167. This rose has been worked with one strand of Gumnut crewel wool.
   1. Form the middle of the rose with three, parallel three-wrap bullions.
   2. Complete the rose by working the following from the middle (in the order given):
      - three, eight-wrap bullions;
      - four, eight-wrap bullions;
      - three, twelve-wrap bullions.

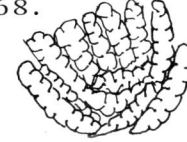

168. This rose has been worked with one strand of tapestry wool.
   1. Form the middle of the rose with two, parallel, three-wrap bullions.
   2. Complete the rose by working the following from the middle (in the order given):
      - three, four-wrap bullions;
      - four, six-wrap bullions;
      - three, six-wrap bullions.

169. These buds have been worked with one strand of Gumnut crewel wool.
   1. Form the buds with eight-wrap bullions. Form the smallest bud with one bullion and the largest with three bullions.
   2. Form the bud 'greenery' with straight stitches.

Fuchsia and Wisteria Garland

Stems, Leaves and Stamens for Fuchsias
Gumnut: beige 643
YLI silk ribbon: 7 mm green 74
DMC stranded cotton: pink 718 (work with one strand only)

170. Beauty of Bath

Flowers and Buds
DMC Medici: white; bright pink 8153

1. Work the top petals in bright pink split stitch.
2. Work the lower petals in white straight stitches.
3. Form the stamens with triple-twist pistil stitches.
4. Work the bud as shown in diagram A.
5. Work the stems in straight stitches.
6. Work the leaves in ribbon stitch with silk ribbon.

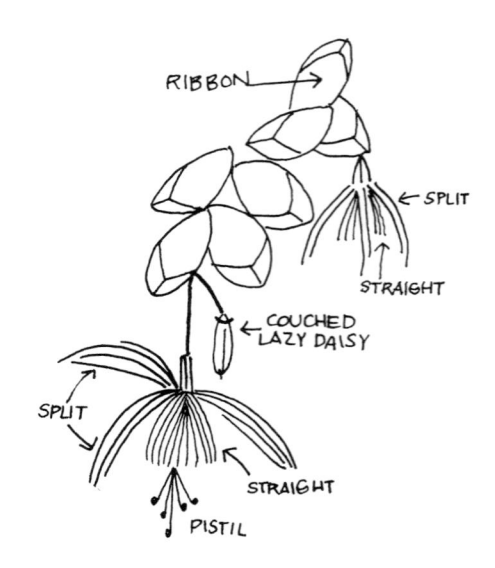

171. La Rosita

Flowers and Buds
Gumnut: peach 825; coral 033

1. Work the top petals in peach straight stitches.
2. Work the lower petals in coral bullion each bullion having between eight and twelve wraps.
3. Form the stamens with triple-twist pistil stitches.
4. Work the buds as shown in diagrams A and B.
5. Work the stems in straight stitches.
6. Work the leaves in ribbon stitch with silk ribbon.

Flowers and Buds
Gumnut: dark purple 277; pink: 052
YLI sparkling organdy: 5 mm pink 6

1. Work the top petals in pink straight stitches (i).
2. Work dark purple, horizontal straight stitches in section (ii). Gather the sparkling organdy ribbon and sew in a zigzag pattern over the horizontal stitches.
3. Work the lower petals in dark purple lazy daisies filled in with organdy straight stitches.
4. Form the stamens with triple-twist pistil stitches.
5. Work the buds as shown in diagrams A and C.
6. Work the stems in straight stitches.
7. Work the leaves in ribbon stitch with silk ribbon.

172. Hazel

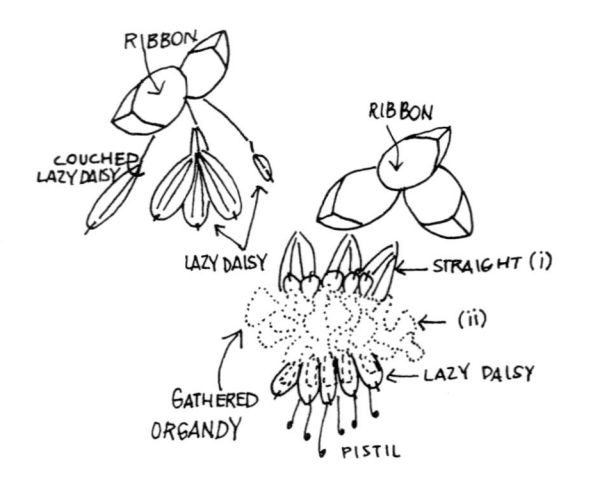

84 Fuchsias

173. Lollipop

Flowers and Buds

Gumnut: pink 054; dark purple 277
DMC Medici: hot pink 8155;

1. Work the top petals in pink split stitch.
2. Work the lower petals in straight stitches.
3. Form the stamens with triple-twist pistil stitches.
4. Work the buds as shown in diagram A.
5. Work the stems in straight stitches.
6. Work the leaves in ribbon stitch with silk ribbon.

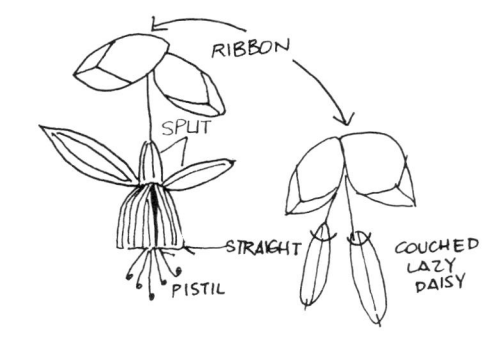

174. Native Dancer

Flowers and Buds

DMC Medici: purple 8794; dark pink 8685

1. Work the top petals in dark pink straight stitches.
2. Work the bottom petals in purple lazy daisies filled in with straight stitches. Complete these petals by working five dark pink straight stitches.
3. Form the stamens with triple-twist pistil stitches.
4. Work the buds as shown in diagrams A and D.
5. Work the stems in straight stitches.
6. Work the leaves in ribbon stitch with silk ribbon.

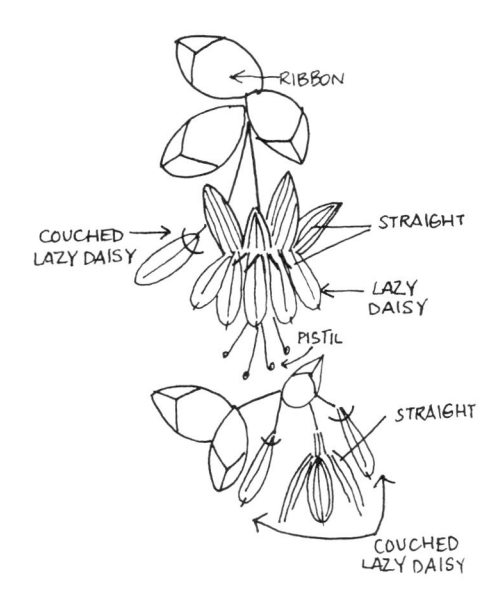

175. Blue Sleigh Bells

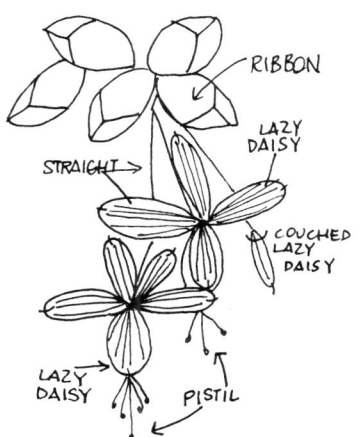

Flowers and Buds

Gumnut: lilac 273; white

1. Work the top petals in white lazy daisies filled in with straight stitches.
2. Work the lower part of the fuchsia in a lilac lazy daisy filled in with straight stitches.
3. Form the stamens with triple-twist pistil stitches.
4. Work the bud as shown in diagram A.
5. Work the stems in straight stitches.
6. Work the leaves in ribbon stitch with silk ribbon.

Fuchsia and Wisteria garland

DMC Medici	Gumnut	Paterna	RoyalStitch	Appletons Crewel	DMC Tapestry	Anchor Tapestry	Appletons Tapestry
white	990	260	NC	991B	white	8004	991B
8153	116	354	NC	354	7151	8488	144
8155	076	353	NC	353	7153	8456	946
8685	058	352	NC	352	7157	8458	940
8794	257	311	NC	456	7017	8596	456
white	**990**	260	NC	991B	white	8004	991B
8132	**033**	955	NC	752	7004	8432	752
8151	**052**	915	NC	751	7132	8482	751
8151	**054**	904	NC	753	7151	8452	753
8896	**273**	302	EW33	452	7896	8524	452
8794	**277**	300	EW30	456	7708	8528	456
8421	**643**	644	EW63	331A	7371	9302	331A
8134	**825**	844	EW10	943	7852	8256	943

86 FUCHSIAS

WISTERIA

176.

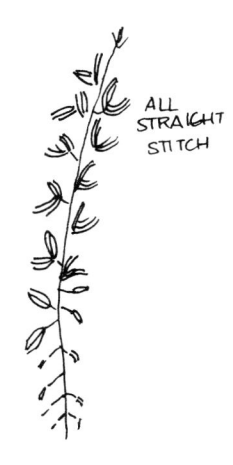

Stems

DMC Medici: light green 8369

Flowers

Gumnut: lilac RQ2

1. Work the stems in straight stitches.
2. Work the flowers in small, lilac straight stitches.

177.

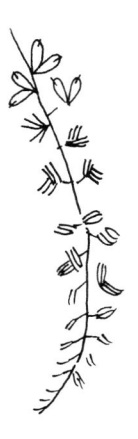

Flowers

Gumnut: mauve R2

1. Work the stems in straight stitches.
2. Work the flowers in small, mauve straight stitches.

178.

Flowers

Gumnut: pink GL4

1. Work the stems in straight stitches.
2. Work the flowers in small, pink straight stitches.

DMC Medici	Gumnut	Paterna	RoyalStitch	Appletons Crewel	DMC Tapestry	Anchor Tapestry	Appletons Tapestry
8369	635	614	NC	353	7369	9014	353
8818	**RQ2**	325	EW23	751	7260	8542	751
8397	**R2**	304	NC	601	7251	8524	601
8896	**GL4**	322	NC	603	7253	8522	603

Stitch Glossary

Back stitch
Up at A, down at B; up at C, down at D.

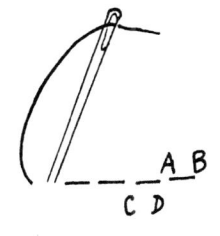

Blanket stitch
Down at A, through to B; have thread under point of needle and pull through; repeat.

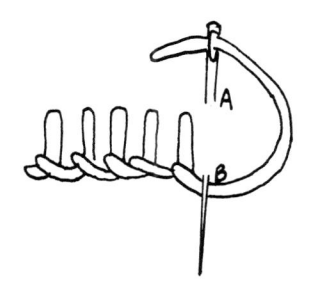

Curved blanket stitch
Work as for a blanket stitch but curve the line of the stitch.

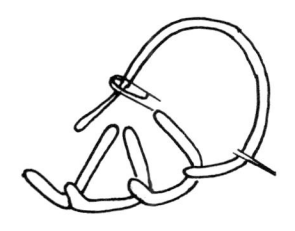

Bullion
Up at A; place and leave needle in at B, out next door to A; place required number of wraps around needle; pull needle through holding wraps; down next to B.

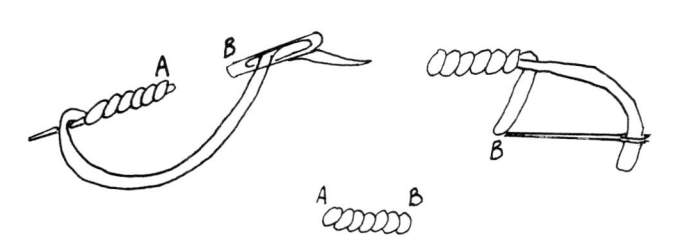

Chain
Up at A, leave a loop; down at B, through to C; repeat.

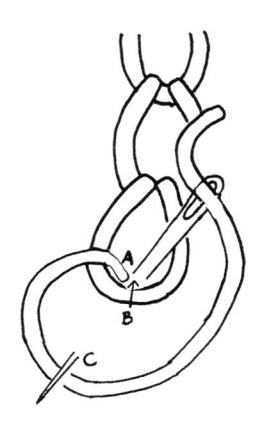

Coral
Make a small 'bite' of fabric at A; leave needle lying at A; take thread over the top of the needle and under the point; pull through; move to B and repeat.

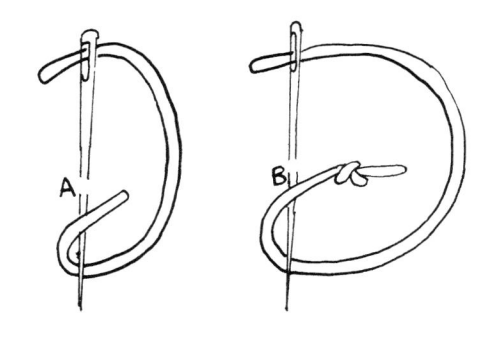

Fly stitch
Up at A; hold thread below C; down at B, up at C; down at D.

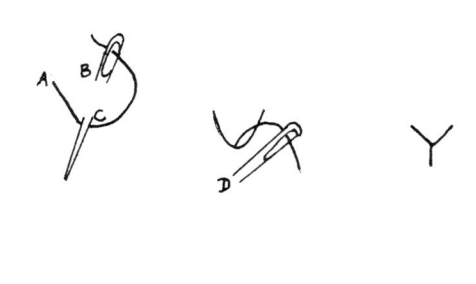

Stacked fly stitch
Work as for fly stitch but vary the size to form leaf shape.

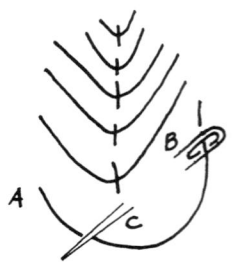

Uneven fly stitch
Work as for fly stitch but make either A to C longer or B to C longer.

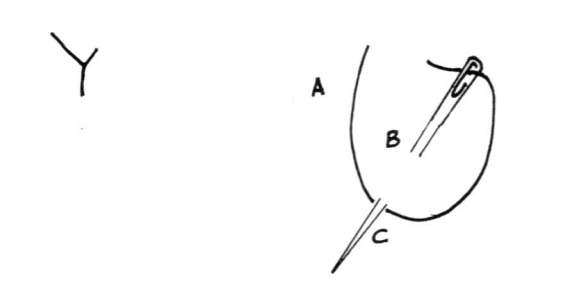

French knot
Up at A; twist thread around the needle; down at B.

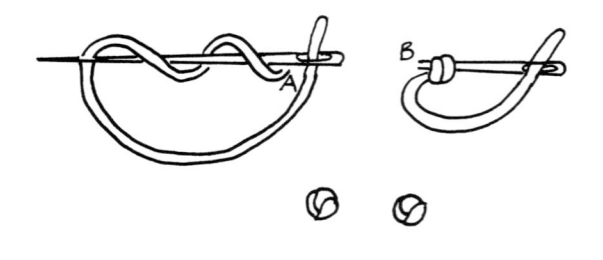

Lazy daisy
Needle up at A, down next door; leave a loop; through to B, down at C.

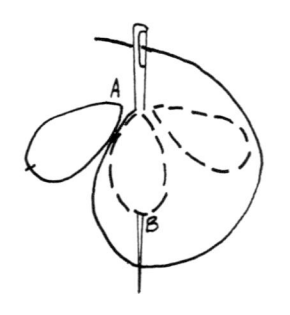

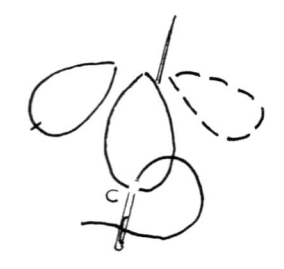

Lazy daisy with straight stitch centre
Complete lazy daisy; work a straight stitch inside lazy daisy.

Double lazy daisy
Work outer lazy daisy first; inner second.

Triangle lazy daisy
Up at A, down next door; leave a loop; up at B, down at C; up at D, down at E.

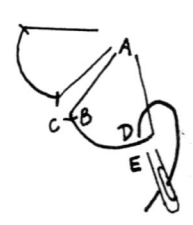

Lazy daisy with straight stitch going over point

Complete lazy daisy first; up at A, down at B (over point of stitch).

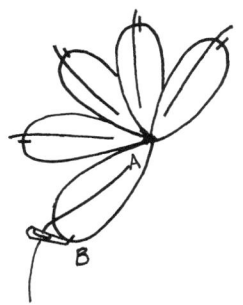

Ribbed wheel

First work the required number of straight stitches for the number of spokes required

Up in the centre; back over and under 1st spoke; back over and under 2nd spoke; repeat until spokes are covered.

Pistil stitch

Up at A; twist thread around needle as if to make a French knot; down at B.

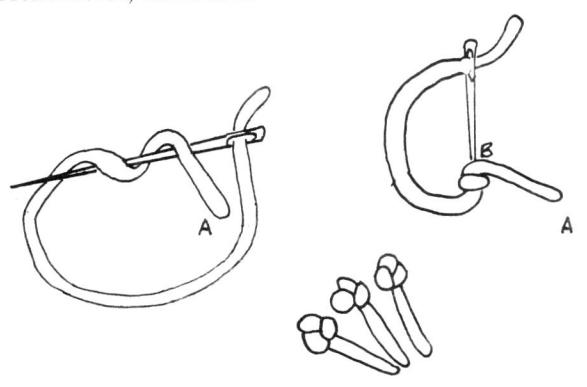

Ribbon stitch

Up at A; lie ribbon flat onto fabric; take needle down at B.

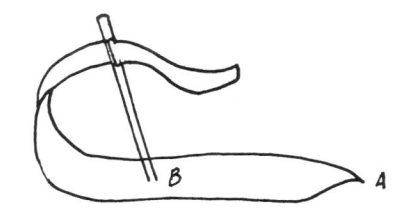

Split stitch

Up at A, down at B; up at C coming through the stitch as you come up; down at D; up through the stitch at E; repeat.

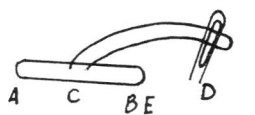

Stem stitch

Up at A, down at B, through to C; repeat.

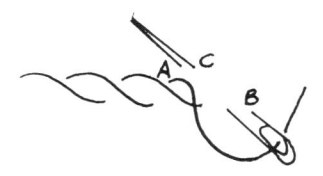

Straight stitch

Up at A, down at B.

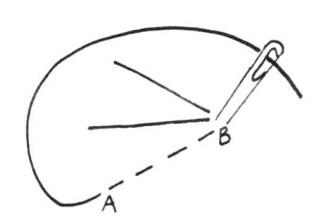

Index of Plants

Agapanthus	35	Flannel Flower	57
Alkanet	36	Forget-me-not	22
Aquilegia	24	Foxglove	33
Astilbe	35	French Lavender	46
Banksia	59	Fritillary	28
Barley	48	Fuchsias	
Black-eyed Susan	63	–Beauty of Bath	84
Blossom		–Blue Sleigh Bells	85
–Blanket Stitch	73	–Hazel	84
–Coral Stitch	74	–La Rosita	84
–Double Lazy Daisy	73	–Lollipop	85
–Whipped Stitch	74	–Native Dancer	85
Bluebell	20	Gentian	24
Boronia	59	Geranium	26
Bottlebrush	60	Gladioli	32
Calla Lily	22	Goldenrod	64
Cardinal Flower	65	Grape Hyacinth	18
Carolina Jasmine	62	Great Millet	52
Chamomile	46	Heather	29
Chicory	48	Hollyhock	32
Chives	43	Hooped Petticoat	19
Christmas Bells	57	Hyacinth	18
Clematis	30	Hydrangea	32
Clover	48	Indian Blanket	66
Cocksfoot	52	Indian Paintbrush	66
Coriander	44	Iris (miniature)	17
Cottage Tulip	18	Iris	21
Cotton Weed	29	Japanese Anemone	37
Crocus	19	Japanese Iris	38
Cyclamen	28	Jonquil	17
Daffodil	19	Kangaroo Paw	57
Dahlia	31	Larkspur	38
Dandelion	32	Lilac	65
Delphinium	33	Lilium	26
Deptford Pink	63	Lupin	37
Dianthus	26	Lythrum	36
Dill	45	Marjoram	47
English Daisy	23	Marsh Mallow	47
Evening Primrose	28	Meadow Grass	51
Everlasting Daisy	61	Michaelmas Daisy	34
False Foxtail	50	Morning Glory	27
Fescue	50	Mountain Pasque Flower	62

93

Narcissus	21	Thistle	31
Pansy	25	Thyme	43
Parsley	43	Tiger Lily	36
Peppermint	46	Trillium	62
Petunia	30	Triple Layer Jonquil	20
Pheasants Eye	18	Tulip	20
Pink Lavender	44	Viola	28
Pot Marigold	44	Violet	22
Primrose	26	Wallflower	30
Primula	24	Wattle	58
Quaking Grass	48	Wheat	50
Queen Anne's Lace	34	Wild Oat	49
Rabbit Orchid	60	Wisteria	87
Ragwort	34	Yellow Grevillea	60
Red Flowering Gum	58		
Rosemary	45		
Roses			
–Back Stitch	79		
–Blanket Stitch	82		
–Bullion (full-view)	81		
–Bullion (side-view)	83		
–Chain Stitch	76		
–Coral & Stem Stitch	79		
–Coral Stitch	77		
–Double Lazy Daisy	80		
–Lazy Daisy	77		
–Ribbed Wheel	80		
–Stem Stitch	76		
–Woven Rose	78		
Rush	49		
Sage	44		
Scabious	27		
Sharp Rush	51		
Shooting Star	64		
Snapdragon	23		
Snowflake	17		
Spider Orchid	58		
Spiderwort	62		
Spotted Knapweed	64		
Sturt's Desert Pea	61		
Sunflower	66		
Sweet Pea	25		
Tasmanian Waratah	60		
Tea Tree	58		
Texas Bluebonnet	64		

Author Profile

Merrilyn Heazlewood is an internationally recognised embroidery designer.

With a wealth of memories and experiences of a contented childhood spent growing up on the family farm in rural Tasmania, Australia, Merrilyn has become a leader in the design of wool and silk ribbon embroidery. Her innovative work has led her to write and publish nine embroidery books which are distributed around the world.

Tasmania's temperate climate has strongly influenced her designs, especially the wide range of seasonal flowers. Her work is noted for its botanical correctness.

For fifteen years Merrilyn owned and managed her needlework retail outlets as well as teaching a wide range of embroidery styles and techniques to students at all levels. With a natural talent to pass on her enthusiasm and love of embroidery, Merrilyn continues to teach extensively throughout Australia and overseas.

Merrilyn's time is divided between Tasmania, where she does her design work, writes and publishes her books, and overseas, where she is in demand for classes and promotion of her books.